All You

Practical Approach to
REIKI

Chetan Chhugani

New Dawn

NEW DAWN
An imprint of Sterling Publishers (P) Ltd.
A-59, Okhla Industrial Area, Phase-II,
New Delhi-110020.
Tel: 26387070, 26386209
Fax: 91-11-26383788: E-mail: mail@sterlingpublishers.com
ghai@nde.vsnl.net.in
www.sterlingpublishers.com

All You Wanted to Know About - Practical Approach to Reiki
© 2002, Sterling Publishers Private Limited
ISBN 978 81 207 2454 9
Reprint 2010

Printed in India

Printed and Published by Sterling Publishers Pvt. Ltd.,
New Delhi-110 020.

Table of Contents

Introduction

Reiki is the name given to the healing energy present in nature.

There is no magic involved, no 'hocus-pocus', nor is there a need to create an altered state of consciousness in order to do Reiki. It is well to remain focused on the treatment, but Reiki will work automatically whenever the hands are applied to the area of need.

Reiki is always present, but we are unaware of it until the contact is made through training, after which it can be received and channelled.

Reiki is not a technique or a method or a process; it just is. In an intellectual sense, Reiki cannot be "taught", the teacher of Reiki empowers the student with the energy being transferred during the four brief ceremonies called "initiations". These initiations open certain inner centres of the body so that the energy can be channelled easily and safely.

After the initiation, the flow is sensed in the hands, being felt usually as warmth, sometimes as a vibration or tingling, and so on.

Since each person is unique, there are individual experiences.

Instruction is given then, for the use of this energy. Specific hand positions are taught for the sake of healing self and others.

The practitioner does not create this energy, but is simply the channel through which it is transferred, and in accepting this role, there is no attachment to results. One does not become a healer; Reiki is the healer.

Reiki is harmless and does not hurt anyone. It will vitalise all forms of life — plants, animals, fish, fowl and humans, from infancy to old age — and it can only do good.

It will work through all layers of clothing, so it is unnecessary for one to disrobe in order to receive a treatment. It will also pass through wood, metal, casts — even rubber. With the second degree training, one does not even have to touch the person being treated, for this energy can be directed to any place at a distance.

Healing chronic conditions will require long-term treatment, as they are of longer standing and have not developed overnight, and much Reiki will be needed to bring the body back to balance.

It will not remove birth defects, nor will it grow a new organ, which has been removed surgically, but it will bring relief from the symptoms resulting from these conditions.

The overall effect of Reiki is to help bring the body into balance so that it can heal itself.

The benefits of Reiki are unlimited. It helps in healing at all levels – physical, mental, emotional and spiritual. It removes physical and emotional blockages and stress and brings about complete relaxation. It cleanses the body of accumulated toxins and helps to get rid of unwanted habits and addictions. With Reiki, one's creative power increases and energy amplifies. It helps to improve memory and become positive. Reiki also helps one to live in peace and harmony with others by helping one overcome anger and fear. Besides, it helps cure insomnia, obesity, lethargy, tiredness and migraine and increases self-confidence.

Other features of Reiki
It is not necessary to study for a long time in order to learn Reiki.

To become a Reiki channel all you need is the attunement. It is passed on from the master to the student. The process of attunement lasts only 5 to 10 minutes.

After the attunement, even if you do not use this therapy for yourself or for others, the energy doesn't diminish or go away. Once you are attuned, you have this energy for the rest of your life.

Concentration is not needed as it is not mind control. You are attuned to cosmic energy, which transcends your mind.

During the therapy, Reiki automatically balances the energy to the correct (required) level.

After being attuned to the second degree, you can send Reiki to somebody who is not physically present there.

Reiki therapy augments any other treatment.

Reiki works whether you believe in it or not.

Reiki raises your consciousness.

Chetan Chhugani

Phone   : (022) 6254345 (Mumbai).
e-mail : c32@vsnl.com; chhugani@yahoo.com
Website : http://www.geocities.com/
          cchhugani/reikibombay.html

History of Reiki

Dr. Mikao Usui is the discoverer of this healing technique which he called Reiki. In his search for the mystery behind the miracles of Christ and the Buddha, Dr. Usui discovered the light of Reiki, which explained to him the various symbols

Dr. Mikao Usui

connected with Reiki. Thus enlightened, he began to practise physical healing in the slums of Kyoto.

Gradually, to add spiritual healing to the physical aspect of Reiki healing, Dr. Usui added to Reiki, five spiritual principles:

1. Just for today, do not worry.
2. Just for today, do not anger.
3. Just for today, have the attitude of gratitude.
4. Just for today, be honest to yourself.

5. Just for today, show love and respect for every living thing.

He also determined not to give Reiki to anyone who did not appreciate it.

After his transition, Dr. Usui's work was continued by his most dedicated disciple, Dr. Chujiro Hayashi, a forty-seven-year-old reserve naval officer. With the transition of Dr. Usui, Dr. Hayashi became the Reiki grandmaster, carrying on this tradition of teaching and healing from his clinic in Tokyo.

But it was a young woman named Hawayo Takata – who herself found relief from multiple ailments through Reiki – who helped to spread Reiki throughout the world and make it as popular as it is today.

Ist Degree

Reiki is a Japanese term, made up of two syllables — "re" and "ki". "Re" means universal and "ki" means life force. So, Reiki means universal life force.

Reiki is the name given to the healing energy present in nature. All of us have access to this energy. When we hit against something accidentally or if an area in our body is suffering from pain, then automatically, our hand goes to that area and we tend to keep it there — this is the body's ancient wisdom. Actually, in doing this, we are channelling healing energy to this area. We have access to this healing energy, but can channel only about 5% to 10% of it. The initiation that is done in Reiki opens up the channel for optimum level of energy, so that we can have access to 90% to 100% of this healing energy and see significant results in our healings.

The channelling of energy need not be thought of as 'mystical'. Just as oxygen is present in nature and our body has the ability to take it in, similarly we have the ability to take in the healing energy. In other words, attunement does not *give* us the *ability* to channel, but *increases* our channelling ability to its optimum.

There are certain energy centres in our body that are responsible for this channelling of energy; they are called the *chakras*. Although there are a lot of *chakras* present in our body, we will restrict our discussion to the seven major *chakras* and two sets of minor *chakras* that are important in Reiki.

The areas where they are present in the body are illustrated in the figure. The *chakras* are conical in shape, connected together by the central channel. At the other end, they open in a circular shape about six inches in diameter. This opening is outside our physical bodies and into the aura (more about the aura is discussed later.)

Out of the seven major *chakras*, five have counterparts at the back of our bodies, i.e. there is the front *chakra* and the back *chakra*. The two exceptional *chakras* are the crown *chakra* and the

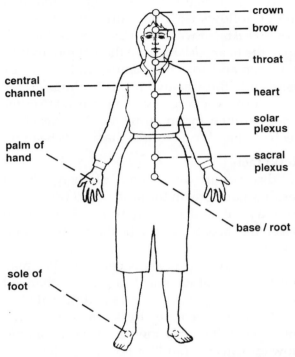

crown

brow

throat

central channel

heart

solar plexus

palm of hand

sacral plexus

base / root

sole of foot

root *chakra*, which face upwards and downwards respectively.

The two sets of minor *chakras* are present in the palms and in the feet.

When we channel Reiki, the path that this energy follows is: from nature it enters our crown *chakra*, moves down the central channel, up to the heart *chakra*; from there it moves into the arms and into our hands; and from our hands into the area that needs healing.

To use this energy, we simply need to (after being attuned by an authentic Reiki teacher) keep our hands on the area that needs healing.

Reiki facts

All diseases are disharmony of energy. Reiki restores harmony in the system (body). This is its way of healing and thus, there is no particular procedure for healing a particular disease.

The healing process is complex. We may not know what chemicals are to be changed inside; but the energy knows and does it all.

This is because Reiki has its own intelligence. It knows how much energy should flow into an area (and for how long). It knows how the healing should be done. This energy is spiritual and, thus, transcends the mind. When we keep our hand(s) on an area to give Reiki, we need not concentrate. It is not mind

14

power. If it were through the mind, then we would have to start and stop the flow ourself. We would also have to direct the energy properly to the affected area and do the healing through our mind. But Reiki does not require all this.

Because we need not use the mind for healing, it can be used for something else simultaneously. This means we can talk, watch T.V., work, etc., while giving Reiki. We can even do our work with one hand and give Reiki with the other. Also, we can give it at any place and at any time. We could be travelling or in our office and still be giving Reiki.

Reiki is an invisible energy. Externally, there is no way to know whether energy is flowing or not. We can only feel it, perhaps in the form of heat in our hand. But remember, the feeling is all in the mind; we may not feel anything in our hand, and the energy might still be flowing.

When we keep our hand on an area that needs healing—the energy flow starts, and we feel some warmth in our hand. This is the most common feeling, although some people feel some throbbing or tingling sensation, or some other kind of 'flow'. When the flow of energy increases, the warmth in our hand will also increase. The flow and the warmth will reach an optimum level. It will remain constant for some time and then, it will start to fall or become less. When the warmth in our hand comes down to the level of our body temperature, it is an indication that the flow has stopped.

Ideally, we should keep our hand on a particular area for as long as we feel the warmth or energy flow. But if we are doing the full body on ourself or on others, it is suggested that we spend about 3 minutes on each area, the reason being that there are about 27 points and 3 minutes on each comes to about an hour and a half. So, if we spend more time on each or any area, we should have that much extra time.

After learning Reiki, we should give Reiki to ourself whenever possible; it is like giving food to the body (as we will learn during the course of this chapter). Some people ask me whether it is compulsory to give Reiki everyday. I tell them that it is not compulsory that we must do Reiki on ourself after completing the course, but it is an ability that we possess, which is not only beneficial but also essential to the body. As I have mentioned earlier, it is like food for our body, for it restores depleted energy. So, we should give it to ourself whenever possible.

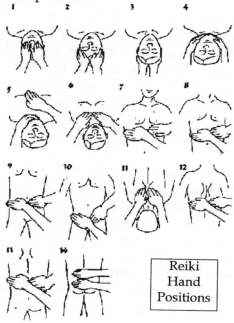

Reiki
Hand
Positions

Now, let us refer to the illustration. What we are really doing while following this figure, is giving Reiki to the entire body. Since the idea is to give Reiki to the entire body, we should not be obsessed with the precise location of each hand position. We can add to or modify them.

It is also not compulsory that we maintain the sequence of these points or that having started doing full body healing, we do all the points in one session. According to the time we have, we can split the full body treatment points into two or three sessions an hour in the morning, then again, half an hour in the afternoon, and finally, another half hour at night.

In case we do not have time to cover all the points in one day, we can do a few points in one day and others on another. Like this, we can do the full body treatment in a matter of a few days. We may even have days in between when we can't do Reiki at all; it doesn't matter.

If we are really, really busy, then we should start doing Reiki when we are lying down in our bed at night, ready to go to sleep. We may be able to do only 4 or 5 points, but that is okay. We are better off than a person who doesn't do Reiki at all.

If we don't find this satisfactory, then, on our day off, we should spare about an hour and give Reiki to the full body. Many people do this.

If we are giving Reiki to an area and we have to get up for some reason, it is alright to remove our hand from that particular area. There is no harm, we can continue after sometime, when we are free. Even if we do not get a chance to get back to that area on the same day, it is okay.

We need not close our eyes or concentrate while giving Reiki. As Reiki flows from the *chakras* in our palms, we just need to keep the palms on the area that needs healing. We should not be bothered about a particular way of keeping our hand, although we follow the practice of cupping our hand while giving Reiki. Cupping means keeping the fingers together with a slight conical shape formed by the fingers and the palm. The reason behind keeping all fingers together is that it gives a feeling of integration to the hand, which helps

19

us to feel more and judge better about what is happening in our hand.

We can try this experiment. If we keep one hand open, with the fingers wide apart and the other hand with the fingers together, we will be able to feel more in the hand where the fingers are together. However, the flow of energy will be the same, whichever way we keep our hand. We do this only for our own judgement.

If we don't practice or use Reiki for a long time, our channelling ability does not vanish. Even if we do not do Reiki for two years, we will still remain attuned to it and when we start doing Reiki again, within a few sessions, we will sense the same amount of flow in our hands. Once a person is attuned for Reiki, he is attuned for a lifetime and needn't get attuned again. Attunement is like a door that is open, and once the door is opened, it remains open.

Reiki points
When we are giving Reiki to an area that has an ailment or a disease, it will require 10 to 30 minutes, or even longer of Reiki healing.

The first 5 points in the full body treatment are called the head points.

If we want to cure headaches, migraine, sinus, weak memory, insomnia (sleeplessness), stress, etc., we need to give Reiki to the head points.

If we want to improve our memory and don't have time to give Reiki to all the 5 head points, then we can give Reiki only to the temples.

Four points, among all the other points, are very important. Almost everyone requires energy at these points. If we are sitting free and can give Reiki, then we should do so for these areas. They are the heart *chakra*, the solar plexus, *hara* and the kidneys.

Hara is the more popular Japanese term given to the IInd *chakra*, i.e. the sacral plexus.

To increase our will-power, self-confidence and self-esteem, we should give Reiki to the solar plexus.

In case of any kind of fear, we give Reiki to the knees.

In cases of suppressed anger, Reiki is given to the upper back, in the areas below the shoulders.

Other things to know in Reiki

- When we start healing others, there are two things that people will ask us even before we start healing them. These two questions are: 1) Will I get completely cured? and 2) How much time will it take?

  These are two questions that no Reiki practitioner can answer. We are just channels of the energy, it is not us who heal. The energy decides the amount and the rate of the healing.

- We may also find that if we are healing two people suffering from the same disease, and both of them have been undergoing it since the same time and with the same intensity, even then, one person may get completely cured in 20 days, while in the other person we may probably see a difference of only 10%. All healings are individual and it is for the energy to decide the way of healing.

There are a few factors, however, that may affect the healings, like, the willingness of the person to get healed, the extent to which the lessons connected with the circumstances have been learnt, and even one's *karma*.

- Reiki practitioners are not healers; they are channels of the healing energy.
- If we are healing a lot of people, we should not think that our energy will get depleted and we will need to charge ourself to heal again. We are not using our energy for healing; the energy is just passing through us. So our energy will never become less while healing. In fact, we might even feel energised.
- Even illiterate people can learn Reiki and use it. It is a practical process and does not require any study or specialised knowledge. People from all age groups can learn Reiki. I have personally taught people of ages 6 to 66.
- A few of my students (who have done the grandmastership course) have attuned the farmers working on their lands, while others have attuned the mechanics who work in their garages. In both cases, the energy is channeled to the objects they

handle with their hands, i.e. the seeds, the soil and even the broken down vehicles.

- Reiki is not a religion, so we don't have to practise any rituals or norms or even give up any practices that we already follow. Reiki is universal, as universal as the oxygen that we breathe.

- Reiki has no harmful effects. Because it is guided by the higher consciousness, it can never cause any harm. When adequate amount of Reiki has gone in a particular area, the flow stops — we cannot force more energy in this area. Even if we have drifted into sleep while giving Reiki, it will not 'overflow' or cause any harm. If the person we are healing has drifted into sleep, we can continue giving Reiki, and the body will still take it. A lot of mothers find that babies and small children can be given Reiki only while they are sleeping because they don't sit peacefully at one place when they are awake.

- Very rarely, there are times when we are healing an ache, and instead of becoming less, it aggravates. This is called a *healing crisis*. It should not be mistaken as a negative reaction; it is a good sign. It only means that the healing is taking place at a rapid rate, and the toxins accumulated in that area over a period of time are being worked upon. This sometimes causes some discomfort and can result in increase in the pain. In these cases, treatment should not be stopped. If the person feels uncomfortable on touching the area, or if the pain increases on keeping a hand on that area, then Reiki should be given without touching that area by keeping the hand about 3 to 4 inches away from the body.

In cases of aggravation, we need to explain to the person what is happening, otherwise he may think we have done something wrong.

- Attunement is a process whereby the capacity of the *chakras* to channel the energy is increased. This is more commonly called 'opening of the *chakras*', but it should be noted that the *chakras* are never closed or opened. These are relative terms. 'Opening'

25

simply means that the capacity of the *chakra* is increased and 'closed' means that it is blocked and that the *chakra* is causing an inadequate flow of energy.

● Reiki should be given to people who have at least some respect for it and also for the time and effort that we are sparing to heal them. After being attuned, we should not catch hold of anybody and everybody and give them Reiki. Just because Reiki can be easily learnt today doesn't mean it is of little value. It is a very powerful method of healing – and also the simplest.

● Normally, it is suggested to have an exchange of energy (mostly in terms of money) whenever we give Reiki. But we are not going to charge our family members or relatives or even friends. We might feel compassion for a stranger who is suffering and might offer to give Reiki. In these cases, if we are really giving Reiki through compassion, then there is no need to charge any money. But if we are not charging anything and don't feel any compassion for our healing or feel obligated to heal, there

26

will be an imbalance of energy. We are giving, but not receiving. Here, the person becomes indebted to us and it is said that the person will have to pay us back some way or the other in future. But because of misconceptions, people take a token of five or even one rupee from everyone they heal. This is not necessary.

Holistic view of the body

In science, we are taught that we are our body and that the body is a collection of chemicals, tissues, etc. But in our day to day life, how many times do we think of ourself as a body, a collection of organs?

Whenever we think of ourself, we always think in terms of our desires and expectations. This is because our bodies are intimately connected to our life events, desires, aspirations, feelings, etc.

This is where the *chakras* play an important role, for they form a link between these daily life issues and our physical body.

There are seven such issues that are important for each human being. They are:

1. Survival.
2. Stability.
3. Will-power (self-confidence, self-love).
4. Relationships (love).
5. Expression (of ideas and emotions).
6. Intellect (ideas, imagination).
7. Spirituality (intuition, guidance, belief in some divine energy).

These are the seven general categories that our life is made up of. And they also form the basis of perfect health. But what is perfect health?

The food that we eat, the water that we drink and the oxygen that we breathe... these form the food for the body. These things produce energy inside our body and get stored in its storehouse. Whenever we move our muslces, speak or perform any action, the energy to carry these out comes from this storehouse. Even thoughts need energy; actually thoughts themeselves are energy. If a person is sitting quietly without doing anything, even then, there is continuous mental activity going on and the person is expending energy. This energy is emotional energy.

To keep our body healthy, we not only need to feed it with food, water and oxygen but also with emotional energy.

This energy comes from our day-to-day life. Each and every event in our life affects us emotionally. With each event, there is a give and take of energy. This is a healthy exchange that is required by the body. A block in a *chakra* means nothing but that because of some reason, there is no healthy exchange of energy through this *chakra*.

The *chakras* in our body connect to the seven endocrine glands in our body (shown in the figure). The energy coming into the *chakra* affects the working of these glands. They produce hormones that act as coded messages, and go to the organs telling them how to function.

On a practical level, this means that the balanced expression of all the life issues will give balanced energy to the *chakras*. This energy will, in turn, assure proper functioning of the endocrine system and thus the entire body.

Now, with this knowledge, we can define perfect health as: having a balanced diet, a good amount of exercise, fair amount of rest and a balanced expression in all the seven issues of life.

This mechanism can be expressed as:

Life Issues ⇔ *Chakras* ⇔ Endocrine Glands ⇔ Physical Body

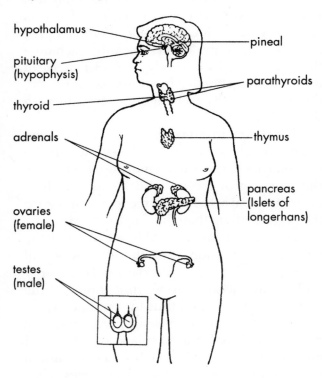

hypothalamus

pineal

pituitary
(hypophysis)

parathyroids

thyroid

adrenals

thymus

pancreas
(Islets of
longerhans)

ovaries
(female)

testes
(male)

Thus, we have stimulus coming from experiences and our inner soul urges. According to the issue to which it belongs, this stimulus, which carries emotional energy, enters the respective *chakra*. For e.g., an event that has to do with relationships will affect the heart *chakra*. This energy will affect the thymus gland and that in turn will affect the group of organs connected with it.

Whether this energy is good or not will depend on how we react to the event. If it is an event that gives us happiness in our relationships, then the effect will be healthy; but if it is an event that gives disappointment, the energy coming from this event through the heart *chakra* will affect this *chakra* in an adverse way and lead to a block if such stimulus is continued over a period of long time.

An event may affect two people in different ways. After witnessing one event, you may disapprove of it while I may approve of it. I may even derive pleasure and satisfaction from it, whereas you may get angry. How we react to events depends on our individuality and conditionings.

The sense organs simply deliver the reality of events; they don't influence or cause any reaction. From the sense organs, the information goes to that part of the brain where we interpret the events according to our perceptions. Then, the reactions occur in our body.

A lot of time, we may not make a conscious response to the stimulus, but our subconscious is aware and brings about a reaction in our body. So, we may be sitting somewhere and find that we have become restless but cannot figure out why; something that is happening in our present situation is causing our subconscious to send this message to our body. These reactions are always happening in our body.

When our long expected desire materialises we feel elated, our body feels light and energetic. But if the same expectation was not fulfilled, we feel depressed. This is simply a practical example of how all external stimuli affect our bodies.

Mechanism of diseases

Before we start to do any healing, we should know the mechanism of diseases. It works as follows:

If we have a problem related to any of the life issues, we will find that most of the day we are obsessed with this aspect of our life. Continuously acknowledging this block will then affect the amount of energy entering our heart *chakra*, and even if we try to get busy and not think of it, we will not be able to hide it from our subconscious and the reaction will be the same. As a result, over a period of time, the energy coming into the heart *chakra* will become inadequate. This will affect the physical body and cause problems either in the chest, lungs, heart or shoulders. This is the disease mechanism.

Healing

Now, to heal this by Reiki, all we have to do is keep our hand over the heart *chakra* and over the area that is affected, and channel Reiki. But the cause of the disease is some event, series of events, some issue or a matter of attitudes. Reiki will also try to rectify these.

Every disease will have a block of energy in the aura (around the physical area that is diseased). When we heal through Reiki, it will not only go inside the physical body and start healing the area, but also work on the energy block in the aura. It will also go into the brain and affect the mental patterns connected with the disease.

So, to heal by Reiki, all we need to do is to keep our hand(s) on the area that needs healing. This should be done for a number of sessions till the disease is completely cured. If we like to keep things simple, then this is what we should do. But if we like to get to the cause of things, or if one is a psychoanalyst or a counsellor, then we may want to adopt the following approach:

On the first session with the person whom we are healing, we should first ask about the disease/ailment and see which area of the body is affected. Next, we should ask about the time the disease appeared.

The answer to the first question will provide us with the knowledge of areas to be healed— we should also include the *chakra(s)* closest to the area(s). With the knowledge of the *chakra*, we will come to know what issues are involved.

The answer to the second question will give us the knowledge of the time when the symptom was first diagnosed in the body. But we should remember that the disease must have started developing well before in the aura, and the event causing this disease happened even before this.

What we are trying to do here is to find the event that has caused this disease. We do this by first seeing the area affected, then connecting the area to the closest *chakra*, giving the healing to the *chakra* and seeing if it is really taking a lot of energy. When we know the *chakra* involved, we know, in general, what issue is involved.

Now, to find the exact cause, we ask the person about significant events that happened at the time. Through my experience, I know that almost all the time, the person will speak of some events which did occur and affected the person mentally and emotionally. Sometimes it is not a single event but a situation that a person has had to put up with.

Suppression of emotion can cause a block in the throat and the heart *chakras*. This is because the expression issue is connected with the throat *chakra* and relationship with the heart *chakra*. Slowly, with each day, this block will increase in intensity because the subconscious knows and acknowledges this suppression which is causing an imbalance of energies in the normal functioning of the *chakras*.

When this energy block becomes very dense, it starts affecting the endocrine glands involved and, in turn, causes a disruption in the normal functioning of organs and glands. Thus, these areas will get affected.

So, the time when the first physical symptom occurs is not the time of the event that occurred. Judging the time can be a tricky thing since it depends on the intensity of reaction (emotionally) on the person.

To make our job easier, let us take some real life examples:

Example 1

Physical symptom diagnosed: A 24-year-old boy had spondylitis since a year.

The doctors had given him medicines, not for curing but only for controlling it. He was forced to do physical exercises for an hour everyday so he could function with minimum discomfort throughout the day. If, some day, he didn't exercise, the stiffness in his back would seriously restrict his movement.

Cause: Death of his grandmother about a year and half ago.

Explanation: He was very attached to his grandmother and when, one morning, his servant woke him up to give him the said news, he was so shocked that he couldn't speak for an hour. His jaw had become 'locked'. Then later with the help of other family members he came out of it and could speak normally.

Because he did not express his grief in any manner, his heart *chakra* became affected. The shock gave him a kind of paralysis and stiffness, which, with time, moved into his upper back, the area at the back of the heart *chakra*.

Example 2

Physical symptom diagnosed: A woman of 58 had arthritic pain in hands, elbows, knees and feet since more than a year.

Cause: About 2 years back, she retired from the job of a school principal. Her son-in-law had expired a year and a half back.

Explanation: Her son-in-law died suddenly at a young age. In his death she saw her own death. She was also not accepting the fact that her son-in-law could die at that age.

Being retired from work she had nothing to do at all, nothing to look forward to. All these factors together, i.e. old age, emptiness, combined with the fear of her own death, caused this reaction in her body.

Arthritis in the legs gives discomfort in movement. Metaphorically it prevents you from moving forward in life.

Example 3

Physical symptom diagnosed: A 26-year-old girl, married for two years had continuous headaches accompanied with heaviness which would also cause her to "blackout" at times.

Cause: Constant worry, disoriented life, trouble in getting over circumstances of past.

Explanation: Before marriage, she was a happy-go-lucky, jolly, gregarious and very sociable person. After constant bickering from her mother over marriage, she finally let her mother decide about getting married wherever she thought suitable. After her marriage, she faced a lot of restrictions and false accusations from her mother-in-law. She was not allowed to have any friends and talk with anybody on phone. When she could bear no more, she left her house and went back to stay with her parents.

Recently, her husband asked her to come back. She agreed on the condition that they would buy a house and stay away from the in-laws. Now, although she has a peaceful life, she is totally disoriented and does not know what to do with her future. She is also bothered by the memory of past incidents. She has consistent heaviness and headaches. Finally, she decided to learn Reiki and see if it could help her.

There was another such case where a young woman was forced by circumstances to leave a very high profile job and take care of her and her brother-in-law's kids. Although she was a good house-wife, she was also an expert in the line of her career. Not being able to express her creativity brought about dullness, worry, suffocation and, finally, she became the victim of the above-mentioned symptoms.

There might be a lesson to be learnt here. In these cases, the 'disease' has come from the circumstances caused by the attitudes of the people, which are inherent in our society. We should be aware of these so as to not to get victimised and be aware that someone else also is not getting victimised by our attitudes. No amount of medicines can cure the effects of wrong attitudes.

Example 4
Physical symptom diagnosed: A 56-year-old housewife has asthma since many years. Whenever Reiki is given to her lungs and heart *chakra*, her upper back (the area below her shoulders) starts paining.

There is relief from regular healing, but the suffocation comes back and she still experiences occasional attacks.

Cause: Feeling suffocated in life, worried about daughter's marriage, feeling of no control over matters relating to her family.

Explanation: This lady's problems come from her early life: financial troubles, looking after her four kids and living with a non-supportive husband.

Her unexpressed anger had accumulated in the upper back and thus every time Reiki was given for her asthma, she felt pain.

The need to make sure that her daughters did not do anything which will debase her respect in the society made her narrow-minded and strict. As a reaction, the daughters started hiding and lying about things. Whenever she came to know about their affairs, she got upset and this gave rise to asthma attacks, and, at times, high blood pressure.

Despite all kinds of medicines for many years, she still continues with the same intensity of disease.

Elaboration of the issues connected with the *chakras*

Ist *chakra*:

The first *chakra* is also called the *root chakra* or the basic *chakra*. It connects to the issue of *survival*. Emotionally, it connects to the 'will to live' and, physically, it connects to the immune system. So, when a person is feeling depressed ('down' or 'low'), the energy in the root *chakra* decreases and the strength of the immune system is weakened. Also, when a person loses the desire or will to live and has no motivation in life, this *chakra* is affected.

This *chakra* connects with the adrenal glands. Adrenaline is one of the hormones secreted by these glands which helps us in a 'fight or flight' situation. Adrenals connect indirectly with motivation, zest, strength, etc. If a person is physically weak, the root *chakra* should be given a considerable amount of Reiki. In cases of emergencies or when people are kept in ICU in hospitals (whatever the symptom), root *chakra* should be given more energy.

If keeping hands on root chakra is not possible or awkward, then the feet should be given Reiki. The minor *chakras* in the feet connect to the root *chakra*.

IInd *chakra*:

The second *chakra* is called the *sacral plexus*, and is more commonly known as *hara*. *Hara* is a Japanese term. It is the area of our 'guts', which has also been called the centre of our body. The second *chakra* relates to the *stability* issue of our life. Stability is connected to creativity and, in a complicated way, to peace of mind. Let me explain this stability-creativity-peace of mind connection. Creativity is the work that we do, and in return we get energy (normally in terms of money). This money helps us with our survival, stability and growth. When we are contended with our work and we know that we are growing in our line of work, we get peace of mind. When our survival, stability and growth are taken care of, it gives us fulfillment. This is how these three things are connected.

But in our society, many people are in a wrong line of work. They are not doing what they have an aptitude for and this causes disruption of peace of mind, giving rise to a constant conflict and discontentment inside. This is also one of the factors of anger.

The work which is in harmony with our aptitude is what I call our 'life-work'. Not doing our life-work results in unhappiness.

The second *chakra* is also the sexual centre. Because of societal pressures, this issue is suppressed, and thus this *chakra* always has less energy then others. It seems shrunk in size.

When we eat food, the basic raw energy is produced in the Ist and the IInd *chakras*. This basic energy is also sexual in nature and needs to be sublimated to change it to creative energy. Sublimation brings this energy into the head (third-eye *chakra*) and the heart *chakra* is connected to the arms and hands. The energy from the heart *chakra* moves into the hands. We do our work with our hands and thus creativity is expressed through our hands. People who are continuously absorbed in work which they like doing are continuously sublimating and using this energy as it is produced in the I^{st} and IInd *chakras*. They remain fresh and light in the body. They also do not feel sexual to the level where this energy becomes burdensome.

There are two *chakras* that connect with the issue of relationships: the heart *chakra* and the *hara*. When we care for and love a person, we are connected to that person through the heart *chakra*. This kind of relationship gives freedom. This freedom lets the person be natural in their expression. But when we relate to a person for our own survival, stability, fulfillment or expectations, then we bond with this person through the *hara*. This binds a person. Here, the person does not feel free. There are conditions put on this kind of relationships. There is a fear for stability and survival for the future attached to this relationship. This is the state of a relationship when a person says, "What will become of me if something happens to you?" This kind of relationship concerns the *hara* and not the heart *chakra*. In many relationships, people feel suffocated because there are energy cords 'binding' that person, which are coming from the partner's *hara*.

When we hear a shocking news (that usually concerns our survival, stability or relations), we feel a kind of hollowness and emptiness in our *hara*, as if something has been torn away from that area. We lose our 'centre'.

The problems in conception also relate to the *hara* (and the root *chakra*). Although there might be a complex combination of issues that are the root of the problem in general, it may be fear of life. When a person is afraid of life itself, how can he/she give birth to a new life? These are also the causes of problems in delivery. The endocrine glands that relate to the *hara* are the gonads, i.e. the testes in the male and the ovaries in the female.

Hara is the stability centre. Stability is a state of being where we have all the needs of survival fulfilled, have a home and a stable source of income besides continuous growth in our field of work. Lack of stability affects the *hara*. Obesity is generally caused because of this lack of stability in life. Normally, obesity comes into this area first. When a person realises that he/she cannot get stability in the external world, they put on weight in the stability centre. This internal heaviness is a substitute for stability.

Obesity does not always come due to the block in *hara*. Many a times it comes from a block in the throat *chakra*, too.

3rd *chakra*:

The third *chakra* is called the *solar plexus*. It connects to the issue of *will power*. There are two 'will' centres in our body — one is the solar plexus and the other is the 6th *chakra*, i.e. the third-eye *chakra*.

The issues of the third *chakra* are will power, self-confidence, self-esteem and self-love. A lot of Reiki should be given to the solar plexus in the following cases:

1. Sensitive Reiki channels who empathise with people whom they are healing, thereby getting affected emotionally, mentally and physically themselves.
2. People who suffer from diabetes.
3. People who suffer from improper blood pressure.
4. People who feel inferiority complex or superiority complex.
5. People who feel nervousness, fear or less confident.
6. People who are dominated by others.
7. Students, for increase in confidence especially during their exams.
8. People who want to get rid of addictions.
9. People who are depressed.
10. People who feel drained of energy in a crowd, or at the end of the day.
11. People with any problem with pancreas or stomach.

The endocrine gland related to the solar plexus is pancreas (the pancreas on the whole does not function as an endocrine gland, but specialised cells within it called the Islets of Langerhans do.)

4th *chakra*:

The fourth *chakra* is the *heart chakra*. It exists in the centre of the chest and not over the heart organ, which is a little towards the left side of the body. The issues related to the heart *chakra* are *relationship, love and compassion.*

Relationships cover a major part of our lives. Relationships here means all kinds of relationships — whether it is with one's spouse, parents, kids, other relatives, acquaintances, friends, etc. Any emotion/thought regarding any relationship, or anything within the relationship, affects the heart *chakra*.

Our way of living today has left many depleted in this *chakra*. Most people require energy at this *chakra*. In cases of lack of love, the back of the heart *chakra* should also be given a lot of energy.

Heart *chakra* should be healed in the following cases:

1. Any problem with the heart *chakra*.
2. Pain in the chest region.
3. Asthma or any problem with lungs.
4. Breast cancer.

5. Person who have experienced a heart attack.
6. Blood-pressure problems.
7. Spondylitis (give more Reiki to the back of the heart *chakra*).
8. Divorce, break-up in a relationship.
9. Other problems in a relationship.
10. In cases of addiction.
11. People prone to anger, and also to those who suppress it.
12. People experiencing blocks in creativity.
13. People who are afraid to give.
14. For peace of mind.
15. To heal anxiety, nervousness (in these cases the *hara* and solar plexus should also be given energy).
16. Any problems with shoulders, arms or hands.
17. People suffering from cancer.

The endocrine gland that connects to the heart *chakra* is the thymus. This gland is closely related to the body's immune system. In childhood, it controls the production of white blood cells, which fight off infections. This gland can be considered as the godmother for the child. Mothers should give Reiki to the heart *chakra* of their young children everyday, for about 10 minutes.

5ᵗʰ *chakra*:
The fifth *chakra* is the *throat chakra*. It relates to the issue of *expression*. Emotions are in the heart *chakra* and ideas are in the third-eye *chakra*. They both get expressed through the throat *chakra*. If the self-expression of a person is blocked, it affects the throat *chakra*. Any part which forms the mechanism for verbal communication may get affected. Any suppression of expression will affect this *chakra*.

A person who has gone through certain painful experiences in the past or is going through one in the present will experience problems in these areas if he/she doesn't share the problems with anyone.

Blockages in expressing issues about one's stability in life affect the thyroid gland and also result in obesity. In these cases, the thyroid should be healed first (*hara* becomes a secondary point in healing).

Problems with the throat may be accompanied by headaches, digestive problems or/and lower backache. In these cases suppression of expression is causing problems in these areas. (Heal the throat *chakra* first and then heal these areas.)

6th *chakra*:

The sixth *chakra* is also called the *third-eye chakra*. The third-eye relates to *ideas, intellect, imagination and mental patterns*. Mental patterns are the conditionings and beliefs that exist in one's mind. Whenever any mental healing is required, this area is healed.

The third-eye *chakra* should also be given Reiki for treatment of headaches, insomnia, stress, to clear fogginess (to get clarity of thought), to increase memory, sinusitis, migraine, if the person is sensitive to light (glare), to help in concentration. The back of the third-eye *chakra* should be healed for digestive and urinary problems.

It should also be given Reiki while healing addictions, relationship problems, worry, tension and for mental peace. It is also helpful in cases where one is healing any disease, ailment or limitation in the body or trauma which has occurred due to some incident/event in the past.

The third-eye *chakra* affects the pituitary gland. The pituitary gland is also called the king of the glands; it sends orders to all the other glands.

As mentioned earlier, there are two will centres in the body — one is the solar plexus and the other is the third-eye. The energy behind our intentions is released from the third-eye *chakra*. It is also an area of intuitive perception, foresight and visualisation. This gland controls the will power, the power of discrimination and sight, hearing and memory. All geniuses have a predominant pituitary gland. This gland also controls the growth of the body. Its dysfunction may lead to making people physically large or dwarfs.

Pregnant women should avoid tension, as this may lead to negative effects on the pituitary gland of the child in the womb, resulting in varying degrees of mental retardation.

If we want to heal people who have a tendency to lie, be disobedient or even steal, then the third-eye *chakra* should be given a lot of Reiki.

Sometimes, dysfunction of this gland can also lead to obesity after childbirth.

Continuous fear affects the pituitary gland and can make a person very weak and timid. Tension and worry disturbs the function of this gland and can lead to high blood pressure and problems in the digestive system.

7th *chakra*:

The *crown chakra* is the seventh *chakra*, located at the top of the head. It relates to *intuition, guidance and spirituality*.

All guidance that we receive as thought, inner voice or gut feeling actually comes from the crown *chakra*. We connect to our higher self through the crown *chakra*. During any form of meditation, this *chakra* becomes very active. In cases of mental retardation, this *chakra* should be given Reiki. In cases of the mind losing synchronisation with the soul (self), and of sensitivity to light (glare), which may lead to headaches, this area should be given Reiki along with the solar plexus.

The crown *chakra* connects to the pineal gland, which also acts like a body clock. It produces a certain hormone, Melatonin, at night. This is a light-sensitive gland, and this is the reason why a lot of people cannot sleep with the lights switched on.

Other important issues relating to the body parts.

1. Eyes are affected when there is a non-acceptance of present reality and when we project our own reality over it. They also get affected because of unshed tears.

2. The ears can get affected if we don't want to listen.

3. The back of the neck is affected when some people or circumstances, keep us from doing things our way. Being obsessed with doing things 'my way' affects this area. It gives stiffness, rigidity and pain in this area.

4. If we are worried about our responsibilities, our shoulders will get affected.

5. If we don't like the work we do (with our hands), then our arms and hands will get affected. Arms and hands can also get affected in relationship issues. Arms are the extensions of the heart *chakra*. They also relate to the receiving and giving within relationships. If we complain that we have

54

to do all the work ourself without the help of others, then also we may hurt our arms and hands.

If we feel that our life is out of control, that we have to suffer because somebody else takes the decisions in the household and we have no authority at all, our arms and hands can get affected.

If we feel we haven't received (back) anything or enough from our children (or even other relations), then the hands might get affected (in this case, the back of the heart *chakra* should also be healed).

6. To increase our memory, Reiki should be given to the temples.

To remove confusion and heaviness in the head, to attain clarity of thought and to make dicisions also, this area should be healed.

Students should be given Reiki here (as well as at the solar plexus), and if there is any nervousness or fear from examinations, Reiki should be given to the knees and the *hara*.

7. Legs are the extensions of the *hara*. Legs help us to move forward towards materialisation of our goals. Our whole leg is divided thus: the thighs relate to the trust in one's own potential. It relates to the feeling of 'I can do it' or 'I have the ability to do it'. The knees connect to the ability to cope with the changing responsibilities that come as we move forward towards our goal. As we move ahead step by step, with change in time and circumstances and the level we have reached, there will be different responsibilities – even unforeseen ones.

Knees are also associated with fear. (In this case also, heal the *hara*.) Knees connect with fear of the future and the fear of death.

The calves associate with keeping oneself focussed and not getting distracted from one's goal. The ankles provide flexibility and balance. People who are extremely imbalanced in life may have these areas affected. Finally, the feet connect us to the ground — the last step in manifesting the idea, which began in the mind. Lack of the ability to materialise our goals means we need energy in our feet.

When we use the phrase 'always building castles in the air' for certain people, they need grounding, and for this, Reiki should be given to their feet.

8. Unexpressed emotions or even tensions can cause energy to go down and lodge itself in the lower back — this problem is associated with the back of the *hara*. (In these cases, the throat *chakra* may also need healing.)

9. In general, the left side of the body relates to the past and the right side to the future. This means that if the left knee has a problem, it denotes fear caused of some past event/circumstance. If the right shoulder has a problem, then this denotes fear of responsibility in future.

Our physical body is the outer expression of how we truly feel inside.

Principles of Reiki

The principles of Reiki were formulated by Dr.Usui when he realised that along with learning Reiki it is important to make a student aware of certain predominant emotions or patterns that keeps one from being healthy and happy.

He formulated five principles of Reiki and preceded each principle with the phrase 'just for today'. This means being conscious of the principle in the present day.

All Reiki teachers have their own way of elaborating and explaining these principles, although the gist remains the same.

What follows is the way I explain these principles:

Just for today, I will have the attitude of gratitude.
It is natural for most of us, at any given time, to focus on the things that we need, things that we don't have yet. When we do this, we are sending signals to our subconscious, affirming that I we do not have these things. By doing this, we are affirming a lack in our lives. Our subconscious listens and obeys. So, it becomes increasingly difficult for us to get the things that we need. A part of our energy yearns for something while another part keeps it away.

If we shifted our inner focus from 'what I don't have' to being thankful for what we do have, and trust that what we need in the future will be provided, this will help us shift from the vicious circle of lacking to the virtuous circle of abundance.

Let me digress here a little. In my first degree sessions, a lot of times people have asked: how to get rid of negative thinking and whether Reiki will help.

Reiki will help, of course. Keep your hands on the third-eye *chakra* and affirm that Reiki helps you in releasing the tendency to think negative.

Besides giving Reiki, if you explored the cause of negative thinking, it will help you release it. The mechanism of negative thinking comes from conditioning. We are conditioned about limitations of our abilities. Negative thinking has its roots in our doubting our own ability.

What is meant for us comes to us when we are relaxed and trusting and not when we are anxious and in the fear that we might not get it.

Now, let us come back to the discussion of the principle. The attitude of gratitude is an ongoing feeling of thankfulness inside us. Some people *say* 'attitude of gratitude' before starting to do Reiki – it should be *felt* and not *said*. It should not be forced, for then, it isn't real.

Just for today, I will not worry.
Worrying is about future insecurity. It is about what might or might not happen.

Worrying is also about the well-being of others, with whom we are attached. It results from the conditioning that events in our life happen without any reason. When we start to accept that there is a greater plan and all things are within this plan, and that all events have experiences in them which are necessary for us, then worry starts to disappear. We start to accept the future and with this acceptance there is no insecurity left – there is only trust.

Acceptance of God and worrying at the same time is paradoxical. Our life is full of such beliefs and patterns which take away clarity of operation. We have to think deeper than we normally do and be aware of such paradoxical or hypocritical beliefs.

Worrying comes from the conditioning that I am separate from the whole existence, that I am not connected to anything and that I have to take care of myself.

But we are all interconnected - even with the plants, sun, air, etc. We need all these to survive. Worrying comes from a feeling of separateness from the universal whole.

Just for today, I will not anger.

When any of our expectations do not materialise, the energy, which was to express itself in this materialisation, turns into anger. One feels irritated and out of control with life, and then, this energy is expressed as anger on a thing or a person. The victim of one's anger may not really be the cause of the anger.

Suppressed anger gets logged into the upper back, into the areas just below the shoulders.

It has been suggested that writing down one's feelings is a good way of releasing pent up emotions. For some people shouting is a good therapy - but this may not be possible to do at home.

It is good to explore the mechanism of anger, to see in each case the cause that has led one to become angry. Sometimes being aware of the cause may release the need to remain in anger.

Just for today, I will be honest to myself.
Honesty here does not mean always speaking the truth. It means being true to one's own innerself.

Although we are always aware of our true feelings in every situation, we sometimes don't listen or pay attention to them. This behavior might also be due to fear or due to lack of courage to act on what we feel.

One can never lie to one's subconscious. At any time when we turn a deaf ear to our true feelings, which might be telling us to take some action regarding a particular matter, our subconscious reacts and our body gets affected.

Just for today, I will show love and respect to every living thing.
This principle talks about respect for life and having compassion. Compassion is a divine quality. It separates us from the beasts.

Before we can have compassion, however, we must have self-love, for without having love for self we cannot share ourself with others.

IInd Degree

With the second degree, you can send Reiki to people who are at a distance and are not physically present in front of you. At this level, you can do healing without the need of bodily contact. You can send Reiki to people across the room, town, country, etc. Distance does not matter.

Reiki does not take any extra time to reach greater distances; it is instantaneous. Physical space doesn't matter. Also, with greater distance the energy does not get weak, it remains the same.

To be able to do distance healing, you need to have two things: (1) you need to be attuned to the second degree level, and (2) you have to make use of a symbol that functions as a bridge—connecting you with the person to whom you are sending healing.

After being attuned to the second degree, whenever you want to do distance healing you must use this bridge.

The symbols are discussed below:

The first symbol

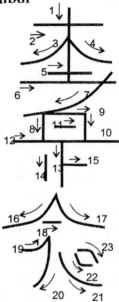

Hon Sha Ze Sho Nen

In the figure, the arrowheads show the direction of drawing and the numbers show the sequence of drawing each line. The actual symbol does not have numbers and arrowheads — so do not include them when you draw this symbol.

64

There are three ways of using this symbol:

1. You can draw it with a pen on a piece of paper.
2. You can draw it with hand in the air.
3. You can draw the symbol in your mind.

The rule with using any symbol in Reiki is that you draw the symbol once and say its name three times.

The name of this symbol is **Hon Sha Ze Sho Nen**. To use this symbol, draw the symbol once and say its name three times.

How to use this symbol for distance healing will be discussed later when methods of distance healing are discussed.

The second symbol

Say Hey Key

Once again, the numbers show the sequence of drawing and the arrowheads show the direction of drawing. Same rule applies to all symbols, i.e. draw the symbol once and say the name thrice. This symbol is called **Say Hey Key.**

The function of this symbol is to bring about emotional and mental healing.

Since emotional healing is connected with the heart *chakra* and mental healing with the third-eye *chakra*, this symbol should be used on these areas.

Use this symbol only when you feel that the person (or yourself) require any emotional or mental healing. You may not need to use this symbol always.

Since I have told you to use this symbol only on the third-eye and heart *chakras*, it may happen that you are healing any area in the body and you feel that this area is affected because of some emotional/mental issue, then use Say Hey Key on the third-eye/heart *chakra*.

The way of using this symbol in touch healing is:

1. If you are giving Reiki to the heart *chakra* and you feel that the person needs

emotional healing, then use Say Hey Key. If your hand is on the heart *chakra*, then simply lift your hand and draw the symbol with your hand over the heart *chakra* and say its name three times, keep your hand and continue giving Reiki.

2. You can also draw the symbol over your palm and say its name three times and keep this hand over the heart *chakra*.

3. You can use any technique given above without lifting your hand, by drawing the symbol mentally and saying its name three times, with the intention that the symbol is sent/given to the heart *chakra*.

The third symbol

Cho Ku Ray

The third symbol is called **Cho Ku Ray**.

It is drawn with a straight line starting from left going right, then continuing down and then spiralling inwards and ending at the center.

The function of this symbol is to amplify energy. It is a very general symbol and can be used anywhere in the body. So it is always used in all the healing sessions. But don't make the mistake of using it on all the points during full body treatment. This would mean you are using it for about twenty-five times in one session — this is a lot of energy and it will make you uncomfortable. Use it on seven or eight main points, where you feel you need more energy.

Some teachers tell their students to use all the three symbol on each point in full body treatment. Please do not do this as this would mean that you are drawing 3 x 25 = 75 symbols. This will make you feel uncomfortable. Also, if you are mentally drawing each symbol, drawing so many symbols will give you a headache.

There is no point in using Hon Sha Ze Sho Nen over your own body, since it is a bridge used for distance healing; although there is only one exception, when you are working with time (past or future). This will be explained later.

You should use Cho Ku Ray over an area that is affected or is taking more energy.

The method of using Cho Ku Ray in touch healing is the same as discussed for Say Hey Key.

Since Cho Ku Ray is an amplifier of energy, when used in conjunction with any other symbol, it amplifies the energy of that symbol.

If you want to use amplified Say Hey Key, then use Say Hey Key along with Cho Ku Ray. You may draw Cho Ku Ray before Say Hey Key or after. You may draw one Cho Ku Ray before Say Hey Key and one after.

Methods of distance healing

Although there are many methods of distance healing, there are two basic methods that are more popular. The simplest of the two is what I have come to call the paper method and the other one is the mental method, where no physical action is required — everything is done mentally.

The paper method

Take a sheet of paper. At the top, write the name of the person to whom you are sending the healing. Below the person's name, draw Hon Sha Ze Sho Nen and write Hon Sha Ze Sho Nen three times.

You may want to draw Cho Ku Ray besides Hon Sha Ze Sho Nen. Write Cho Ku Ray three times. In case you want to do any emotional/mental healing, then also include Say Hey Key.

Below these symbols, write the result that you want. This is usually written in the form of affirmations. For e.g., if you are healing the heart, the affirmation will be 'The heart is completely healed'. After you have prepared your paper, simply keep both hands on the paper and give Reiki. Keep your hands for as long as you would like to. Ideally, the minimum time is fifteen minutes.

After your healing session is over, keep the paper in a safe place; you can use the same paper in your next healing session, there is no need to make a new paper again. Use this paper for as long as you want to continue healing. After the person is healed or when you want to discontinue, simply tear the paper and throw it away. Some superstitious people may want to put it in the water (not in the sink or toilet but in a lake, pond, river or sea). Please don't burn the paper.

If you are healing two or more people, use separate sheets for each person.

If you have made many sheets, for e.g., you are sending distance healing to five people, then you may find that you don't have enough time to give Reiki to each one of them. In this case, you can simply fold the individual sheets of paper and put them all in one small box (any kind of box) or a small purse or a pouch. Then, give Reiki to this box everyday and Reiki will go to all the intentions named inside. This method is popularly called the *Reiki box*.

The mental method

The mental method is where the whole procedure of healing is done through visualisations.

1. Visualise the person you want to heal. If you have not seen the person, then you can mentally say the name of the person.

2. After visualising, draw Hon Sha Ze Sho Nen mentally and say the name of the symbol three times.

3. Now visualise the person again and surround the person with white light. (Here white light represents Reiki energy.)

4. Now, you may draw Cho Ku Ray mentally over the entire person and say the name of the symbol three times.

5. Now, if you want to heal a particular area in the body, move your focus on this area. Surround this area in white light and draw Cho Ku Ray. Say the affirmation(s) relating to this area/problem. For example, 'The pain in this area is reducing, the swelling has reduced, this organ/*chakra* is completely healed', etc.

6. After doing this, move to the next area and repeat the same procedure. When you have finished with all the areas that need healing, again visualise the entire person. You can again draw a Cho Ku Ray for the entire person, say any affirmations and this ends your healing session.

7. There is no ritual for ending your session. When you have finished, simply open your eyes get up and do your normal work.

8. You can do this technique any place at any time.

9. If you are doing this at home, then you may want to raise your hands in beaming position while you are doing distance healing with this method. In the beaming position, you can visualise white light coming out of your palms and going to the person or an area in the person. You can also draw Cho Ku Ray over your palms. The advantage of this step is that you may feel an amount of energy in your hands. By doing this, you come to know how much energy is required or has been taken by that area. (If you don't feel anything, it is not a cause to get worried.)

Other methods

- You can do distance healing by using the photograph of the person whom you want to heal. The photograph can be kept between your hands. Mentally, draw Hon Sha Ze Sho Nen and say the name three times. Do the same with Cho Ku Ray and channel Reiki for about fifteen minutes.
- You can keep the photograph in front of you and keep your hands in the beaming position. Mentally, draw Hon Sha Ze Sho

Nen and Cho Ku Ray (same as above) and beam Reiki for about fifteen minutes. You can also draw Cho Ku Ray on both palms of your hands.

- If you want to use the physical touch method, then you can use a soft toy or a pillow. Assume it to be the person whom you are healing and do full body treatment of the pillow. You will need to use the symbol Hon Sha Ze Sho Nen, as this is distance healing. You can additionally use Cho Ku Ray and Say Hey Key as required.

Whatever method you use, all methods will have three essential steps: (1) Intention (whom you are sending the healing), (2) The ' bridge' — Hon Sha Ze Sho Nen, and (3) Sending healing.

Using distance healing procedure for intentions

Till now, we were discussing healing for the physical body. Using distance healing procedure we can also give energy to intentions. Reiki works when your intention is to help somebody for growth in life. For e.g., you can send intentions for the safety of people, for helping people get rid of addictions, habits and phobias, and for resolving mental patterns formed in the past, which are causing some limitations in the present.

All these various types of healing are discussed in the following sections.

Other uses of the three symbols
Cho Ku Ray

1. Besides amplifying healing energy, Cho Ku Ray is also used for clearing spaces. By spaces we mean rooms, entire houses, offices, factories, hospitals, etc. We want to clear a space for various reasons: if someone has died recently or has been ill in that place, if a place has been kept locked for a long time, if there has been arguments in that place or if you feel a dampness in that place.

   If you are in that room/house which you want to clear, simply draw a big Cho Ku Ray and say Cho Ku Ray three times. Bring your hand in the beaming position. Say affirmations. For e.g., 'This Cho Ku Ray is clearing the energy in this room and is filling it with divine energy' or 'Let this room be filled with divine energy, which will help create harmony, peace, positivity and good health for all people in the house'.

If you cannot bring your hands in the beaming position for whatever reasons, you can just sit with eyes closed and visualise energy coming out of the third-eye *chakra* or the heart *chakra* or both.

2. Cho Ku Ray can also be used for protecting people and things. Visualise the person/thing that you want to be protected and surround it with white light. Draw Hon Sha Ze Sho Nen and Cho Ku Ray, also say the names of these symbols three times. Affirm that this Cho Ku Ray is present in the person's aura and is providing protection to him/her.

One session of such a healing would provide protection for about twenty-four hours.

Say Hey Key
In general, Say Hey Key is used for emotional and mental healing, which means you can use it in any sort of emotional/mental distress, such as nervousness, fear, depression, anger, sadness, etc. This symbol is especially useful

76

in healing relationships, healing addictions, improving memory, curing phobias, etc.

1. To improve memory, keep your hands on your temples, mentally draw Cho Ku Ray and Say Hey Key, and say the names of the symbols three times. Say affirmations like 'My memory power is increasing, I can recall and retain information very easily'.

2. For healing relationships, if you are using the paper method, then write the names of both the persons involved in the relationship. Below their names, draw all three symbols and write their names three times. Then, write affirmations, for e.g., 'The disharmony between them have been resolved. They both have a harmonious, loving, caring and nurturing relationship.' After preparing your paper, keep both the hands on the paper and give Reiki.

   If you are using the visualisation method, then visualise both the people together or say their names. Draw the bridge, i.e. Hon Sha Ze Sho Nen, and then give Reiki. While giving Reiki, use Cho Ku Ray and Say Hey Key to bring about emotional and mental healing. If you have more time, then you can proceed and draw Cho Ku Ray and Say Hey Key over the third eye and the heart *chakra* of both the people and say the affirmations.

If you are healing a relationship, which has gone sour over a long period of time, then this will take a lot of healing sessions.

Many people have found out that no matter how much they give Reiki, certain relationships never heal. This has to be accepted, it is for everybody's good that things remain as they are. But in some cases, people have experienced miraculous results.

If you are healing a minor disharmony in a relationship, then it might take only a session or two to heal.

Divorce is a situation where healing for the relationship should be done individually. If two people are to separate or have been recently separated, then you should project healing especially on the front and the back of the heart *chakra*, and front and back of the *hara* and the solar plexus. These areas get depleted in these cases. You can use an affirmation like 'I have the strength and power to be independent. I feel no need for any emotional dependence on the other'.

3. Using Say Hey Key to heal addictions: Write your name (or the person's name) on a piece of paper along with the unwanted habit. Draw all three symbols and write their names three times. Hold the paper between your hands and treat it with Reiki. This will send Reiki to your mind and emotions that relate with the unwanted habit and will begin healing them. Give Reiki to this paper everyday. You can carry the paper with you and if you feel the unwanted compulsion coming up during the day, take out the piece of paper and give it Reiki.

4. If you want to lose weight, write your name on a piece of paper. Draw all the three symbols and write their names three times. Write an affirmation or a phrase like 'healthy weight loss' and give Reiki to this piece of paper. You can also do this before each meal. With time you may find yourself eating less or eating only healthy food.

Hon Sha Ze Sho Nen

Till now we have discussed the use of this symbol to bridge us through space. This symbol also works with time.

We use it to heal the past and the future. We want to work with the past in these cases: if the person you have been healing is experiencing some limitation/disease which is a result of some event experienced in the past; a person might be undergoing trauma or emotional distress as a result of a recent event; certain behavioural pattern which is limiting, coming from a memory which was formed when the person experienced a particular event in the past.

In all these cases, we want to get rid of such patterns and for this we do 'past' healing. Phobias are also such 'patterns'.

We work with the future when we want to send some help and energy to others or ourselves for some accomplishment in the future. You can also empower goals through this method. People have sent Reiki for the following: helping their kids during exam time, for results, interviews, journeys, protection, negotiations, reaching on time, healing the earth, etc.

People have also done this for goals and possessions. One thing you should note is that giving Reiki for possessions won't get you anything and everything. Only those things will come to you which will help you in your creative expression, growth, contribution and good of others. Things will come to you when the right time has come and you have the energy equal to what that thing is worth.

Many people get carried away with using Say Hey Key. They think they can use it to control people or even get back from people what they owe them. This is almost impossible to achieve. Reiki is for healing and not for manipulation. It doesn't work this way.

Here are some examples of working with past and future.

Past
When you are healing someone by touch and want to do the healing for the past, keep your hand on the third-eye *chakra*. Mentally, draw Hon Sha Ze Sho Nen and affirm that the memory of the event be resolved (if you don't

81

know the event, then just say that the root cause of this condition be resolved). Then, mentally draw Cho Ku Ray and Say Hey Key to do emotional and mental healing.

In the case of healing a phobia, use the same procedure and appropriate affirmations relating to the phobia.

If you are doing distance healing for the past, then the steps for this method will be as follows: (1) visualise the person or say his/her name. (2) mentally, draw Hon Sha Ze Sho Nen (3) mentally, draw Cho Ku Ray and give Reiki (4) now, say the affirmations and draw Hon Sha Ze Sho Nen again, requesting this symbol to help in releasing and curing the phobia.

If you want to do past healing for yourself, then follow these steps: think of a particular issue you want to heal. Then, mentally, draw Hon Sha Ze Sho Nen. Now think about the cause of this issue, which might be an incident in the past. Say affirmations to release this pattern from the memory. Use Say Hey Key and Cho Ku Ray and again repeat the affirmations.

Future

You can use the bridge to send Reiki into the future. If you know that you will be involved in an important activity in the future, and you know the date and time of the event, you can send Reiki to the event so that it will be there to help you when the time comes.

You can also send Reiki to empower your goals. If you have been blocked in the achievement of a particular goal, it usually means that there is something to heal before you will be able to achieve it.

Give your goal a name and write it down on a piece of paper, or just describe it — if dates are involved, write them on the paper as well. Then, draw Hon Sha Ze Sho Nen and Cho Ku Ray and write their names three times. Give Reiki to the paper for twenty minutes or more each day. Continue to actively work to achieve your goal. You will find everything working much better. If the goal is in harmony with your higher good, you will achieve it.

If you are really serious about your goals and are willing to work hard and dedicate more time at giving Reiki, then following is the method that you can use.

1. Take a sheet of paper, write down each goal and the necessary details. Number each goal.
2. Every morning on waking and every night before sleeping, give Reiki to this sheet of paper for 15 minutes.
3. While doing so, mentally visualise each goal and emotionalise it, i.e. imagine the feelings that you would have on accomplishing this goal. Do this for each goal.
4. You can also use the bridge and Cho Ku Ray with each goal. The above-mentioned method is a combination of positive thinking, mind control and Reiki.

Programming with Reiki

Someone needs Reiki say, at 3 p.m. tomorrow, and asks you to give Reiki, but you know that you are going to be busy at that time. In this case, you can give Reiki now, with the intention that it will go to the person tomorrow at 3 p.m. Or, if you do not know the exact time, then you can mention that 'tomorrow at whatever time the particular event begins'. This method is called programming with Reiki.

Group distance healing

When more than one person is sending healing to a particular person, it is called group distance healing. The group may be sending the healing at the same time or at different times, they may be present in the same place or they may be at their respective homes. Usually, this is done in an emergency.

Healing circle

Four or five people sit in a circle with their left-hand in the receiving position and the right hand in the giving position (in the receiving position your palm is facing up and in the giving position your palm is facing down). The person on your left will have his right hand on your left-hand and your right hand will be on top of the left-hand of the person sitting on your right. All of you will do distance healing for a particular person and when you have finished, you can open your eyes and release hands. In cases of emergencies, group healings have been very effective.

Healing the dead

This does not literally mean healing the dead. We are healing people who are attached to people who are dead. There are cases where people have some limitation or disease as a result of being attached to person who is no more. The person may be attached in either a positive or a negative way. Positive way means that the person cares for and is missing the dead person.

Or the deceased may have done some wrong and now the person whom you are healing may be harbouring revengeful feelings toward him. This is being attached in a negative way.

In this case, ask the person whom you are healing to visualise the person who is dead and communicate whatever he wants to. In this way, the weight on the heart and the mind will slowly start to release. This kind of healing, however, will take a lot of sessions.

IIIA Degree

The IIIA Degree gives you additional tools for healing. There are some healing techniques, some more symbols, knowledge of role of colours in healing and some reference material that is given in this level.

Usually, there are one or two symbols taught in this level. But there are masters who also have other traditional Reiki symbols. I met a Reiki master from France once, who told me that there are about hundred traditional Reiki symbols. Most of these symbols are lost, but many masters around the world have a few special symbols which they may or may not share with other masters and students.

I have been lucky enough to have got about fifteen of these additional symbols from my master. When I got these symbols, I was told that only masters could use them. But when I gave them to a friend of mine who was not a master, she got excellent results in her healings. That was the time when I decided to share them with others too. So I put in an advertisement in the *Life Positive* magazine to share these symbols.

When I begin my IIIA Degree seminar, many a times I start the session with these symbols, and at other times, I start with what is called the master's symbol (also called Di Ko Myo).

The master's symbol

The master's symbol is shown below. It is called thus because no Reiki attunement is done without this symbol.

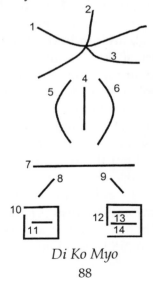

Di Ko Myo

This symbol should be sparingly used for healing. It is mainly used in attunements. Use the master's symbol only in the following two cases:

1. If you have been healing somebody for a long time but you see no significant changes.

2. If you are beginning to heal someone, who has had many diseases since a very long time.

To use it, simply draw it over an area where you are healing by touch. If you are healing from a distance, then either draw it mentally or on paper, along with Hon Sha Ze Sho Nen and Cho Ku Ray.

Exercise for energising your hands

Hands can be energised before doing full body treatment on your self, before healing others, before giving Reiki to the Reiki box or before doing distance healing. There are two exercises for energising hands.

There is a simple technique for energising your hands.

Sit comfortably with hands resting on your knees, in the receiving position (with palms

89

facing up). Visualise a beam of white light coming from above; see it enter your crown *chakra*. Maintain this focus for a few minutes. You are energising your crown *chakra*. Now move your focus to your palms. Visualise two beams of white light coming from above and charging your hands. After a few minutes, you will feel your palms either heavy or warm. You can also draw Cho Ku Ray on both your palms. Now your hands are energised. Use this energy to heal yourself or others.

For people who like to work with visualisations and colours there is one more technique for energising their hands.

Again, sit in the same position as described above. Visualise a beam of white light entering your crown *chakra*. Maintain this focus for a few minutes.

Take it down the central channel till the heart *chakra*. See this light turning pink and energising the heart *chakra*.

In the same manner, again, see white light coming from above and entering your crown *chakra*. Take this light down the central channel to the throat *chakra* and see this light turning blue.

Once again, see white light coming from above and entering your crown *chakra*. Now take this light down the central channel to the third-eye *chakra* and see it turning indigo.

Bring your hands (in cupped position) up to the heart *chakra* and see the pink light filling your hands.

Now, take them gently in front of the throat *chakra*, see the blue light fill your hands and mix with the pink light.

Next, bring your hands in front of the third-eye *chakra* and see its indigo light blend with the energies already present in your hands.

This procedure will greatly amplify the energy in your hands. You can do this every morning, as this would keep your hands charged throughout the day.

With your energised hands, you can heal yourself and others by putting them in between your hands. 'Between your hands' means keeping your hands 6 inches apart, with palms facing each other. Now visualise all the people you want to heal in between your hands. You can simply draw Hon Sha Ze Sho Nen and Cho Ku Ray. If you have more time, you can individually work with each person, using particular symbols for each individual and saying relevant affirmations.

Energising the *chakras*

Following is a small technique that can be used for aligning and energising your *chakras*. You can also do this on the days when you are not able to do full body treatment on yourself (but do not *substitute* it for the full body treatment).

This exercise is done in a standing position. Keep your hands in the receiving position. Close your eyes. Take a few deep breaths to relax yourself. Now, visualise a beam of golden light entering your crown *chakra*, energising it. Take this beam through all the *chakras*, into your knees and then to the *chakras* below the feet, and finally, into the ground. Feel the clarity and lightness in the central channel. This exercise is also excellent for grounding yourself.

(You need to ground yourself when there is a lot of mental activity and your mind is pondering over a lot of things).

Reiki meditation

The essence of this meditation is to mentally focus on the four symbols, i.e. Di Ko Myo, Hon

Sha Ze Sho Nen, Say Hey Key and Cho Ku Ray.
Ideally, this meditation should be done when
you are totally relaxed.

METHOD:

1. Sit comfortably in a quiet place, with your
   hands in receiving position. Close your eyes
   and take three deep breaths. Imagine
   yourself filled with golden light (you can
   also imagine the outline of your body
   which is filled with golden light).

2. With your eyes still closed, draw Di Ko Myo
   in front of you with your right (or dominant
   hand). Say its name three times (you may
   also choose to draw it mentally).

3. Now, see the symbol in gold. Hold the
   image for about five minutes. Do not worry
   if your mind drifts to some other thoughts.
   Just be aware that your thoughts have
   drifted, but finally return your focus back
   to the symbol in front of you (you will get
   better with practice).

   (For people who cannot visualise or find
   it difficult to do so, draw the symbol on a
   piece of paper, let your eyes focus on it and

93

relax. Then, close your eyes while retaining the image.)

4. After about five minutes, see the symbol moving into a field of golden light above you. Bring your attention back in front of your eyes.

5. Repeat steps 2 to 4 using Cho Ku Ray, Hon Sha Ze Sho Nen and Say Hey Key.

6. After meditating on all the symbols, you are not centred and charged with creative healing energies.

You may end your meditation here, but if you have time and want to do distance healing or send energy to your goals, you can continue.

State your goal silently to yourself. Create a picture of it in your mind. See yourself having already accomplished it. Visualise the four Reiki symbols around it, with Di Ko Myo on top, Cho Ku Ray on the right, Say Hey Key below and Hon Sha Ze Sho Nen on the left of the picture. Hold this image in your mind for several minutes or longer, with the thought and feeling of accomplishment. Do this for each goal or healing. When you are finished with the image, state, "If this be possible within

divine love and wisdom, then let it be so."
Then, send the image up into the field of light
above with the feeling of fulfillment. Accept
the idea that the process is complete and that
your goal has been established.

(For people who cannot visualise or find it
difficult to visualise, simply write out the goal
or healing on a piece of paper stating that it
has been achieved, along with the four Reiki
symbols, and hold it between your hands.)

Crystal grid

Crystals are also called clear quartz. We make
use of crystals because they have healing
qualities, they amplify energy and can also be
programmed.

You may want to make use of the crystal
grid when you want to give Reiki to something
that is really important for you. It can also be a
case of emergency. In either case, you would
want to give Reiki all the time, but this is not
practically possible. This is the reason why we
make use of the crystal grid.

Crystal (Reiki) grid is a structure of charged
and activated crystals which you use to send
energy to your intentions. After you charge

your crystals, the crystals continue to send healing energy to your intentions while you are away at work.

Of course, this healing energy going to your intentions won't be as intense as your own healing energy and you also need to charge the grid everyday.

To create your Reiki grid, you will need eight crystals. When you first get your crystals, you need to cleanse them as they would have been affected by the thought energies of the people who have handled them. Because crystals can be easily programmed, they get affected by the thought energies of people who touch them.

You can clear or cleanse them by placing them in salt or salt water. Take a bowl of salt or salt water and immerse the crystals in it. Keep them in the bowl overnight, or for about 24 hours. Say a prayer over them after they are placed in the salt, asking that they be purified for your highest spiritual purpose.

Next, you must prepare a place for your Reiki grid. It could be an altar or a sacred place in your home or a desktop or shelf.

Take your crystals out of the bowl, drain the salt and wash them under fresh, running water. Dry them and place them between your hands.

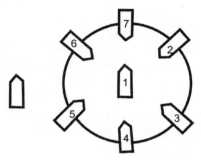

Now you have to activate them. This is achieved by bringing your hands in front of your heart *chakra*. You are channelling Reiki from your hands and with your heart *chakra*, communicating with them, requesting them to help you in your healings.

You can also draw Cho Ku Ray on the palm of your hands before you start to charge them. Now, you can say the following prayer or make one yourself:

'I dedicate these crystals to universal purpose. From this moment on, I undertake to utilise its energies to benefit all living things. For I am one with the creative source, and therefore, one with all life forms. In that which I am, I now activate the life energy within these crystals, in order that its force may be utilised to serve universal purpose.'

After you have charged the crystals, from the eight crystals, select one that seems the strongest (usually the biggest). This will be your master charging crystal. Then, place six of the crystals at equal points around a circle (about 12 inches in diameter) pointing inwards. (Refer to the figure.) Place the last crystal in the centre, pointing at one of the other crystals.

After the crystals are in position, do not move them, as this will weaken their energy connection. The master crystal is to be used to keep your Reiki grid charged. But you must also charge the master crystal regularly. Charge it with Reiki the same way as the others.

After charging the master crystal, charge the grid with it. This is done in the following manner.

Hold your master crystal in one hand. Point it towards the central crystal (the crystal in the centre of the grid). Hold it in this position for a while. You can visualise energy i.e. Reiki coming out of your hand and being amplified by this master crystal. After being amplified, it is going towards the central crystal and charging it. Hold it in this position for about 30 seconds or longer.

Now go to the next crystal in the circle. You can move in any direction, clockwise or anti-clockwise. After charging this crystal, go back to the central crystal and again charge it. You are establishing the connection of all outer crystals with the central crystal.

Next, go back to the last crystal you had charged in the circle, charge it again, and then, go to the next crystal in the grid. After charging this new crystal, again go back to the central crystal and so on.

If all this sounds confusing, then you can refer the figure and follow this sequence:
1 - 2 - 3 - 1 - 3 - 4 - 1 - 4 - 5 - 1 - 5 - 6 - 1 - 6 - 7 - 1.
In this way, your crystal grid is charged. You must charge it everyday. If, on some day, you don't have enough time, then just keep your hands over it in blessing position, draw Cho Ku Ray and give Reiki for few minutes.

You can use this grid to do healing for yourself, empower intentions and also heal others. You can keep your Reiki box in it too. Whatever you keep, for example, photos of yourself or others, piece of paper with an intention written on it or even your Reiki box, can be kept anywhere within the grid. You can also keep this at the centre below the central crystal. If you want to keep the Reiki box in the centre, then you can keep the central crystal inside this box.

Psychic surgery
Psychic surgery is not really a surgery but an intensive form of aura clearing.

If you know that you are very sensitive and feel weak in the solar plexus, then do not do this technique. Also, this technique cannot be performed at a distance. The person whom you are healing should be physically present.

Negative thought energy, which is usually composed of negative thoughts and feelings, blocks the flow of life force and is the cause of diseases. This non-physical negative energy forms clumps of a particular shape and lodges itself in and around the physical organs, the *chakras* or in the aura. It can be removed using this technique.

1. Before you start this procedure, you should be aware of the physical areas affected in the body. Besides, if you are aware of the mental issues relating to the problem, it will help you in your healing.

2. Have the person sit on a chair. Move behind and draw Di Ko Myo on both your hands. Do the same with Cho Ku Ray. Draw Cho Ku Ray down the front of your body for protection. Then, draw Cho Ku Ray over your heart and crown *chakras*.

3. Extend your "Reiki fingers" by pulling on your physical fingers and imagine you are pulling them out into the air about six to eight inches long. Pat the ends of your extended fingers and imagine you can actually feel them. Draw Cho Ku Ray on the ends of the fingers. Do this on both the hands.

4. Ask that the healing take place within divine love and wisdom, so that the highest good is created for all concerned.

5. Draw Cho Ku Ray over the area where the block is located.
6. Reach and grab the negative energy with your extended Reiki fingers and pull it out and release it upwards. Use your perception to guide you in how you pull it out.
7. Care should be taken while removing the negative energy, do not inhale deeply too close to the area (of the block). When you release the negative energy, prefer to exhale.
8. Continue to pull out the negative energy for several minutes. As you do so, you will feel a change in how the area feels. This means you are making progress. Try pulling from different angles and sides of the area. Allow yourself to be guided by your intuition as to what to do and how to do it.
9. After continuing for about four or five minutes, ask the person how he or she is feeling and if they perceive any change in the shape of the negative energy. If the shape is gone, you are done with this part.

If it is still partially there, then continue to pull the negative energy out until the person reports it is completely gone or has been replaced with positive energy.

10. If you find that even after several minutes the negative energy is still present, you will need to communicate with the area to find out what needs to heal. To do this, draw Say Hey Key on the area, hold your hands on the area and talk directly to the area, asking for guidance from it. Ask if there is a lesson that must be learned for the negative energy to be release.

11. After receiving and acting on this information, continue the additional psychic surgery, pulling out the negative energy and asking the person to report the results.

12. Sometimes all the negative energy is released in one session, while at other times, the process of release only gets started and continues on its own for several hours or days.

13. The area should be treated with Reiki afterwards, to fill it with healing energy. Use Cho Ku Ray to seal the treatment.

14. Then use the symbol, Raku, to break the connection between you and the person. This is done in the following manner: draw Raku three times with your hand in the air between you and the person and repeat its name three times. Retract your 'Reiki fingers' by pushing them back.

Raku

15. You may continue with full body treatment using all the hand positions.

General treatment guide for healers

In the IIIA Degree course material, I also include a general treatment guide, which is a ready reference for the Reiki healers. The following table shows the necessary points to heal for a particular disease or ailment. As mentioned, these are the *necessary* points for healing, so you may need to include other points also, as required by the individual case of healing.

Aging	Full body
Allergies	All head points, lungs, kidneys.
Arthritis	Solar plexus, liver, spleen, *hara*, kidneys, affected area.
Asthma	Refer allergies.
Back pain	*hara*, abdomen.
Back injuries	Full back, sides of neck.
Bell's palsy (facial paralysis)	Eyes, temples, cheeks, under the jaw, behind ears.
Bleeding gums	Head points, sides of mouth.
Brain tumor and damages	More time on head points.
Broken bones	Treat on the casting.
Bronchitis	Refer to asthma and allergies.

Burns	Place hands over the area till pain vanishes.
Cancer	Full body, additional 30 mins. on the affected part.
Circulation or blood problems	Feet, knees, upper thighs.
Cold	Head points, lungs, solar plexus, *hara* (3 days treatment needed).
Cuts	Seal the opening to stop bleeding, treat often.
Deafness	Ears
Detached retina	Eyes, back of head.
Diabetes	Solar plexus.
Drug addiction (overdose)	Adrenals, use Say Hey Key on the third-eye *chakra*.
Epilepsy	Head points.
Fever	Heart, solar plexus, *hara*, legs, lungs.
Food poisoning	Heart, solar plexus, *hara*, kidneys.
Fracture	Refer broken bones.

Frostbite	Adrenals, affected part, full body.
Hangover	Head points, heart, solar plexus, *hara*.
Headache	Head points, heart, *hara*.
Head injuries	Head, adrenals.
Heart attack	Heart, solar plexus, shoulders, *hara*.
Heart problems	Same as above.
Hiccups	Diaphragm.
Infection	Whole body treatment.
Laryngitis	Throat.
Hearing and memory	Ears, temples.
Obesity	Thyroid/*hara*.
Parkinson's disease	Full body, more on head, afflicted area.
Pregnancy	Abdomen area.
Throat	Place hands over the sides, chest.
Tongue	Soles of feet, big toe.

Tonsils	Cup hands over jaw for 20 mins.
Varicose veins	*hara*, upper thighs.

Healing with colours

Every *chakra* has some specific energy. Each energy is represented by a specific colour. These colours are on a higher spectrum than what our eyes can see. All the *chakras* together have the colours of the rainbow. Given below is the list of the *chakras* and the colours represented by each:

Root *chakra*	Red
Hara	Orange
Solar plexus	Yellow
Heart	Green
Throat	Blue (sky blue)
Third-eye	Indigo (dark blue or blue-black)
Crown	Violet

There are two ways of healing through colours. One: whatever *chakra* you are healing, simply use the colour of that particular *chakra*, and two: after getting thorough knowledge of the characteristics of each colour, you will know what colour to use under each situation. For example, if you know that a characteristic of blue color is to give peace and calm, you will use this colour to heal anger in a person.

But before we discuss the characteristics of each colour, we must know how to use them in healing.

Using colors in healing

1. If you are healing by physical touch and want to use colours in healing, then simply project the colour on the area where you have kept your hand. By 'project' is meant mentally visualising that colour going into that particular area. If you find this complicated, just visualise this colour in your mind with the intention of sending this colour to that area. If you are a person who finds it difficult to visualise, then just have an intention in your mind that you want Reiki to heal by this colour in this area.

2. If you are doing distance healing and want to use colours in your healing, then during your third step of distance healing procedure (i.e. after you have visualised the

person and drawn the bridge, and are now projecting white light/healing on to that person and are saying your affirmations), you can project a particular colour on a particular area or the whole person. Again, if you cannot visualise, just affirm that you are sending this colour.

3. If you want to have the influence of a particular colour in your life, you can use that colour in your lifestyle, i.e. start wearing clothes of that colour, use things that have that colour, etc.

Characteristics of colours

Red:

Red stimulates the physical body to respond to direct action. Strength, courage, steadfastness, health, vigour and sexuality are all attributes associated with the colour red. It can assist in overcoming inertia, depression, fear or melancholy. It is a great aid to those who are afraid of life and are inclined to feel like escaping. Red is power. It is a great aid to those who are afraid of life, fire, zest and drive. It is passion, courage and excitement. It supplies energy and motivation necessary to reach and accomplish goals.

Orange:

It is a warm and stimulating colour, although lighter than red. Orange is a happy, social colour. It stimulates optimism, expansiveness, emotional balance, confidence, change, striving, self-motivation, changeability, enthusiasm and a sense of community. It is flamboyant, warm-hearted, tolerant and sociable.

Yellow:

Yellow stimulates the intellect and assists communication. It is associated with mental discrimination, organisation and attention to detail, evaluation, active intelligence, academic achievement, discipline, administration, praise, sincerity and harmony. Yellow gives heightened expression and freedom. It is good for concentration and clarity of thought. It is also associated with good luck.

Green:

Green stimulates feelings of balance, harmony, peace, hope, growth and healing. It is found everywhere in nature, symbolising the abundant, replenishing forces of the universe. This is a very good colour because it is restful and healing.

Blue:

Blue is the first of the cool spectrum colours. It stimulates inspiration, creativity, spiritual understanding, faith and devotion. Blue allows for gentleness, contentment, patience and composure. It is also effective in reducing pain. A warm, light-blue bedroom is good for relaxing a hyperactive child. Blue is also excellent for a meditation room or any other room where you want to have a feeling of peace pervade the entire atmosphere.

Purple:

The effects of purple are calming, soothing and comforting. It is associated with psychic awareness and intuition. When a person chooses purple as a favorite colour, he is usually abstract, inspired, trusting in future, and able to tune into the world of others. Purple stimulates our spiritual perspective and intuition. It is so powerful that it is suggested not to paint an entire room in this colour. It can be diluted with white paint to make a soft shade of lavender or violet. This is excellent for meditation room or for a room where you do healing.

White:

White encompasses all colors. Its effects on our being are divine realisation, humility and creative imagination. It can also be purifying. It has the energy and the power to transform the focus of the imagination. White leads us towards higher spiritual attunement and divine love. It is purity and perfection.

Black:

Black is the realm of the visionary and dreamer. It is introvert, whereas white is extrovert. It is constricting, whereas white is expanding. Black is the darkness of the winter, where life lies dormant and in germination. Out of the blackness comes new life. Our day begins and ends with darkness. There are no bad colours. Black focuses attention into the inner world.

Some examples of use of colours in healing are as follows -

Using red colour

Healing someone for depression when the basic life force is down or low. Since basic survival is in the root *chakra*, this *chakra* is affected when a person is depressed. The colour of the root *chakra* is red, so you can heal it through red colour. The root *chakra* connects to the adrenal glands; so you must also heal this area and can do so by projecting red colour to this area. A depressed person will always feel low in self-esteem, confidence and will power. These issues connect to the solar plexus, so you must also heal the solar plexus.

The colour of the solar plexus is yellow, so use this colour on this *chakra*. Now you have three points which you are healing i.e. root *chakra*, adrenals (kidney points) and the solar plexus. If you want to heal the root *chakra*, you can alternatively give healing to the feet—the minor *chakra*s in the feet connect to the root *chakra*, so the healing will go there.

What we normally refer to as mental or even emotional depression calls for healing on the third-eye *chakra* and/or the heart *chakra*. Be a judge yourself and see what kind of healing the person needs. If you decide to heal the heart, then you should spend a good amount of time on the back of the heart *chakra*. The reason for this is that, whenever we feel we are not loved enough, it is that *chakra* that is depleted of energy.

In some cases, healing the shoulders along with the heart *chakra* may give some relief to the person.

If you decide to heal the third-eye *chakra*, then use Say Hey Key sparingly. Instead, use Katsel Chen (symbol no. 15). Do not use blue colour on a person who is depressed. Blue is a passive colour, while the person who is depressed is already passive (at least in most cases).

Note: People who have done Karuna or Tera-Mai Reiki should avoid using Mara symbol on a person who is depressed. This symbol is used for grounding. The depressed person is already feeling low or grounded, so please don't ground him more.

Using blue colour

When you are healing people for asthma, you can project light-blue colour to the whole person or the chest area. Although the colour of the heart *chakra* is green, you are using blue colour to give peace and pacification.

After healing with the blue colour for some time, use green colour for heart and lungs.

In cases of asthma, concentrate on lungs, heart *chakra* (especially back of the heart *chakra*) and you will also need to heal the head point. Also see if the person needs energy on the shoulders.

You can also include the crown *chakra* and say an affirmation like, 'I request Reiki and higher-self of this person to give guidance for expression and release of suffocation, and heal any mental patterns related to this disharmony.'

If you have been told not to give Reiki on the crown *chakra*, then refer to the note on this in the chapter on misconceptions in Reiki.

If you want peace of mind, then light-blue colour should be projected around the head region and also the heart *chakra*.

You may also heal the solar plexus and the *hara* for peace of mind, but do not use this colour here. Simply give Reiki. These additional areas also need healing because when peace of mind is absent, then there is a need of energy in the solar plexus and the energy of *hara* is also dispersed and scattered.

Light blue colour also helps in reducing pain. So you can use this colour whenever you are working on pain in any area of the body.

If you are healing someone who has a lot of anger, you should always use this colour. It will help in reducing the anger. (Never use red colour on a person who has a lot of anger.)

Blue colour works instantly on situations where a person (or more than one person) is experiencing anger.

I will give you an example of one experiment that I did and got excellent results. One day, while travelling in the bus, the bus-conductor and a passenger got into an argument. The argument went on and became a very heated one. This was disturbing everybody in the bus. I intended to send Reiki to both of them, so I closed my eyes, drew the bridge and again intended that healing should go to them. Then, mentally, I drew Cho Ku Ray, projected blue colour on them and continued to send Reiki. Then, I used Say Hey Key with Cho Ku Ray on the third eye and heart *chakras*

of both of them. I used a few affirmations like —
'They are both quiet and peaceful now.' I also
sent Reiki to the back of both the persons' heart
chakras. After about five to seven minutes, there
was peace and quiet in the bus.

In cases of anger, you must heal the heart
chakra also, because if the heart *chakra* is full of
energy, the person will feel no need to get
angry.

In case of anger in a diabetic person, heal
the solar plexus also.

Actually, if it were possible for all of us to
have the heart *chakra*, solar plexus and the *hara*
always full of energy and completely healthy,
we would never feel the need for anger, lack of
confidence, depletion, depression, negative
attachments, fear or hatred.

Using yellow colour
Yellow is mainly used for two areas; one is the
solar plexus, since this is the colour of this
chakra, and the other is the head region. From
the characteristics of yellow colour, it is clear
that this colour gives clarity in thinking. So, if
you want to clear a foggy or confused mind,
use this colour.

118

Also, when you are planning some project, use this colour for the head region as it helps in paying attention to details.

The yellow colour that you use should be lemon-yellow.

Using green colour

Green is a healing colour. You can use it for the heart *chakra* or anywhere else for healing.

You can also project this colour in a place and provide a healing atmosphere. For example, if somebody is ailing in the house or the hospital, you can fill the room with this colour. Prefer to use light green.

Using white colour

White stands for purity and humility. People who are very sensitive and have weak will power should make minimum use of white, as this will make them vulnerable to psychic attacks. The same applies for those very few people who experience some discomfort on their own bodies while healing others. White gives expansiveness and lightness.

Using black colour
Never project black on to others. This colour is not used in healing. The characteristics of this colour have been discussed only for knowledge.

15 symbols
Although people who are attuned to the second degree can use these symbols, I prefer to teach them in IIIA Degree. This is because second degree is the first time when people get introduced to the symbols and including these 15 symbols will be too much to learn. I also feel that with the IIIA Degree attunement, the person will be more empowered to use these symbols.

These symbols are : Ki Yin Chi, Hang Seng Dor, Mil Qu Zu, Jal Jin, Biru Kai, Yoshi Te, Furu Pyo Sho, Jin So Gen, Tse Ne Dong, Chi Hai, Senz Tan, Zen Kai Jo, Michi Ka Ro, Samye Meldru and Katsel Chen.

Symbol No.1 **Ki Yin Chi**
(for prosperity)

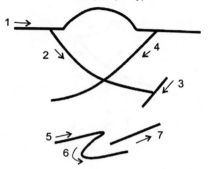

Symbol No.2 **Hang Seng Dor**
(for removing blockages and difficulties)

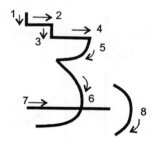

Symbol No.3 **Mil Qu Zu**
(to remove scarcity)

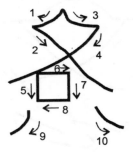

Symbol No.4 **Jal Jin**
(for self-expression)

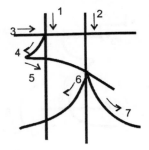

Symbol No.5 **Biru Kai**
(for love)

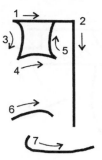

Symbol No.6 **Yoshi Te**
(for relationships)

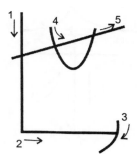

Symbol No.7 **Furu Pyo Sho**
(for meditation)

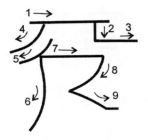

Symbol No.8 **Jin So Gen**
(for peace in the family)

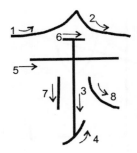

Symbol No.9 **Tse Ne Dong**
(for happiness and smoothness)

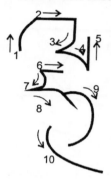

Symbol No.10 **Chi Hai**
(for new ventures)

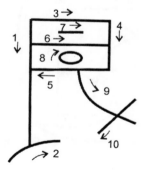

Symbol No.11 **Senz Tan**
(for victory)

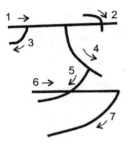

Symbol No.12 **Zen Kai Jo**
(for abundance)

Symbol No.13 **Michi Ka Ro**
(for harmony)

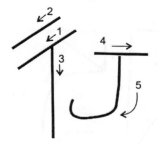

Symbol No.14 **Samye Meldru**
(for peace)

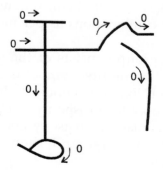

Symbol No.15 **Katsel Chen**
(to remove depression)

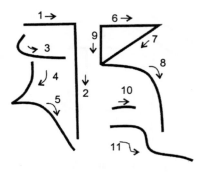

A few of these symbols are used for similar issues; so I like to group them, although there can be many combinations as per individual needs.

The first group consists of the symbols No.1, 3 and 12. The first symbol is used for prosperity and No.12 for abundance. If you are using the symbol for prosperity but perceive scarcity in that place, then use symbol No.3 to remove scarcity first and then use the prosperity symbol.

If you are going to give Reiki for only one session, then use the scarcity symbol first and then the prosperity symbol. But if you are going to heal over a period of time, then use the scarcity symbol for a few days and then the prosperity symbol.

The symbol for abundance can always be used with the prosperity symbol, even in cases where prosperity is present.

The second group of related symbols consists of No.5 and No.6, both of which work with relationship and love emotions.

The third group of related symbols consists of No. 8, 9, 13 and 14, i.e. for peace in the family, happiness and smoothness, harmony, and for peace.

Just because I have grouped these symbols does not mean you have to use them together. I only do this to make understanding easier.

Some ways of using these symbols are:
1. You can use all of these symbols over the full body.
2. Few of these symbols are used for places or even goals. In these cases, visualise the place or the goal and draw these symbols.
3. Few of these fifteen symbols can be used in specific areas of the body. For example,

symbol No. 4, Jai Jin, which is used to help in self-expression can also be used on the throat *chakra* or on the mouth or on tonsils.

4. Don't be worried about the pronunciation of the names of these symbols.

5. Cho Ku Ray can be used with all symbols to increase their energy.

Detailed explanation of the use of each symbol

No. 1 Ki Yin Chi

This symbol is used for prosperity. It can be used for yourself, another person or even a place. It works in both touch healing and distance healing.

A note for those who are disappointed after using this symbol: This symbol does not directly bring money, but it might bring opportunities, or make you aware of your abilities, or even the blocks in your prosperity.

No. 2 Hang Seng Dor

This symbol is used for removing blockages and difficulties. It is a very general and useful symbol. It can be used in almost all cases of healing. You can use it on diseases, emotional, mental and spiritual issues, and also for blockages in accomplishing your goals.

No. 3 Mil Qu Zu

This symbol is used for removing scarcity. Scarcity is a state of affairs where the expenses seem more than the income, or wherein you put a lot but do not get as much in return.

The scarcity symbol can also be used by farmers who feel that a particular plot of land/ soil is not giving enough produce (and then it should be used with the symbol for abundance). This symbol can be used for homes, offices, factories, etc. and even on people.

No. 4 Jai Jin

This symbol can be used for people who have their emotions suppressed or repressed. Thus, it can also be used for past healing (discussed in IInd Degree). Use this symbol in cases of asthma, diabetes, lack of confidence and for any problem with the throat/thyroid. In cases of tonsils also, do past healing. This symbol can be used on the whole person or the throat *chakra*.

When you perceive that a person has a lower back pain and is in a situation where he/she cannot express certain things, then use this symbol.

No. 5 Biru Kai

This symbol can be used to surround yourself with the light of love. It can also be given to places to keep them energised with love energy. You can also use it for healing the heart *chakra*, in cases of breast cancer or heart attacks or any other problems with the heart organ. People have been disappointed when they have used this symbol for attracting love in their lives by using it on someone they fancy. Reiki never works for manipulation. Only if it is for the betterment of all concerned will it work.

No. 6 Yoshi Te

You can use this symbol for healing relationships. It can also be used specifically for the heart *chakra*.

No.7 Furu Pyo Sho

This symbol should only be used on self, before going into meditation. Simply draw this symbol mentally and say its name three times.

No.8 Jin So Gen
This symbol is used for peace in the family. You can use it when there is some disharmony among members of the family. (You can also use the procedures for healing relationships.) You can also use this symbol to "keep" the peace in the family. You can either use a family photograph or the paper method, or mentally visualise the whole family. You can also use it on the house.

No.9 Tse Ne Dong
This symbol helps bring happiness and smoothness. It can be used for healing relationships, for new ventures, places, for journeys, for peace of mind, etc.

No. 10 Chi Hai
This symbol is used for new ventures. It is to be used just before or after beginning a new venture. It can be used for any kind of venture, i.e. a business venture, a new domestic project or for any new beginning. You can use either the paper method or the visualisation method.

Use it on the person as well as the project. You can also help others by using this symbol for their projects.

No.11 Senz Tan
The symbol can be used for success in interviews, tests, negotiations, business deals, or even for exams. For using it on self, just draw the symbol mentally and say its name three times. The symbol is basically for helping you in achieving success in all your ventures and projects.

No.12 Zen Kai Jo
This symbol can be used whenever you are using the symbol for prosperity. It can be used for self, others and even for places.

No. 13 Michi Ka Ro, and No. 14 Samye Meldru
These are general symbols that can be used for bringing harmony and peace. You can use them on people, places, to heal relationships, for ventures, for stress, for the heart *chakra*, etc.

No. 15 Katsel Chen
Whenever you are healing for depression, use this symbol for the entire person.

IIIB Degree

This is the level where all the four attunements are taught, i.e. attunements of I, II, IIIA and IIIB degrees. In this level, the student is attuned to the IIIB level, which empowers him/her to attune other people.

Usually, people who want to teach Reiki take this course. But I have also had students who don't want to teach and still do this level for curiosity, knowledge, spiritual evolvement or with the intention of attuning family, friends, etc.

There is a lot of confusion between the concepts of mastership and grandmastership. I will try to clear these here. Some teachers call the IIIA degree mastership and the IIIB grandmastership.

According to me, all the attunements should be taught in the IIIB level. This is what I follow, and to avoid confusion, I use the term grandmaster for the IIIB level.

I do not wish to reveal the attunements in this book as I want to maintain the tradition of secrecy and sacredness of Reiki and of course, to avoid misuse.

If you do learn the IIIB level, then the first thing you should do is to attune all your family members, so that they can do Reiki without being dependent on you. Till what level you should attune them is up to you.

Some of my students have had to hide from their families that they do Reiki as their family members do not believe in it. Then, there have been cases where a person is not allowed to do any course, especially the daughters-in-law of the house. These young women come to learn Reiki to help them ease the suffocation at their respective homes.

Guidelines for people who are aspiring to become teachers of Reiki:

- The procedure of attunement is a guaranteed procedure. Do not ever feel after attuning someone that the attunement was not done.
- The attunement is a very subtle process, involving very sublime and refined energy; do not expect to feel anything during the

attunement. A thunder bolt will not strike you and you will not see any colours.

- You are going to get students who do not believe in Reiki. In such cases, I simply tell them they are fools to pay for something that they don't believe in.
- If you are going to be a teacher, you must have your concepts and misconceptions cleared. The chapter on misconceptions will help you in that.
- When I attune, I prefer to have the initiate sit facing either in the north or the east direction.
- Distance attunements are not possible. The initiate must be physically present in front of the teacher to get the attunements. Only *mahatmas* (great souls) are known to attune (raise *kundalini*) from a distance.
- People fancy seeing the aura and are after anybody and everybody who will help them see it. But even if you succeed in seeing it, the prominent thing in a person's aura are the blocks. Do you really want to see everybody's blocks throughout the day? If you are a professional healer, then, maybe

yes. But even after seeing the blocks you are going to do nothing but heal them, which you can also do in the Ist degree level through physical touch.

- When you decide to teach, you will be bothered about the question of how much to charge. I decided my fees by going into meditation at night and asking Reiki to help me decide about the right amount for each level. After doing this for a few nights, one day, I sat down and decided the fees, and the feeling in the body agrees with it. This is the way to decide.

- You should limit your course to essentials and avoid adding irrelevant things. If you have about three to five students, there is really no need to extend your seminar for two or three full days. You may need this much time only if you are including some therapeutic, guided meditations in your seminars.

- Crystals, pendulums, vastu, etc. do not really form a part of traditional Reiki, but some teachers choose to include these.

- If you are ready to teach but feel there are some challenges that keep you from teaching, just trust in Reiki and request it to help you.
- All Reiki teachers are not doctors, but some doctors choose to do Reiki also. We must all try to enhance our knowledge of anatomy.
- Some people think Reiki teachers are psychic. Few of them may be, but most of them are ordinary people like me.

Questions, Doubts and Misconceptions in Reiki

There are quiet a few things which have been misunderstood or misinterpreted in Reiki. For example, when we say, 'Reiki is not given but taken,' what we really mean is that the area which is being healed takes the energy according to its requirement.

And when we say, 'Reiki is given only when asked for,' it does not mean wait till a person asks for it, otherwise do not give. To clear this type of misunderstandings and doubts which are often raised in my sessions, I am including this chapter.

1. Remove watches, belts, ties and jewelry when doing Reiki.

This is not a rule; these things do not impede the flow of Reiki. The reason why this is said is that if you are a professional healer, you'll prefer to be as light as possible with loose, cotton clothes. Because you are working with a subtle energy, you want to be comfortable and with minimum of discomfort. So, avoid jewelry, belts, etc.

2. Should the eyes be closed while giving Reiki?

It makes no difference whether you keep your eyes closed or open while giving Reiki because you don't have to concentrate. You might want to close your eyes if you want to pay more attention to the feeling in your hands.

If you are attuning, then the person being attuned should close his eyes because this makes him receptive and also aware to the subtle feelings that may take place during the attunement. If the eyes are open during attunement, your energy might be distracted and you can not focus within.

3. Is it necessary to have a carpet on the floor while attuning?

Whenever a person feels energy in excess and is burdened, the way to get rid of it is by channelling it to the ground. To do this, the person keeps the palms on the floor for some time so that the energy goes into the earth.

Because of this, people might think that energy is taken by the earth, and if you are getting attuned keeping your feet on the floor, it might result in the energy flowing into the ground. But this is not so. You need not be bothered by these things.

Attunement can be done anywhere at any time and in any kind of clothing—even in shoes. It is not necessary to have a carpet on the floor while attuning. The person can very well keep the feet on the floor. But if you choose to have a carpet, that is okay too.

4. In what sequence should the three symbols of the IInd degree be used?

Some people are told about the sequence of using these symbols and also to use all symbols in all healings. There is no such thing as the right sequence and you may not even need all the three symbols in all the healings.

If you are doing distance healing, then you must use Hon Sha Ze Sho Nen first. Then use Cho Ku Ray to increase the energy. Use Say Hey Key only if you think that the person needs emotional or mental healing.

If you are healing through touch, you don't need Hon Sha Ze Sho Nen, except if you are working with the past or the future. (This is described in the chapter on the second degree.)

5. Draw spirals and balance the energy in spine (in the Ist degree).

These two small procedures are almost obsolete now, as they really serve no purpose. There is no need for balancing after the treatment.

6. While giving Reiki, the fingers should be kept together

The energy flows out of the minor *chakras* in the hands, although you feel it all over your hand. Thus, it doesn't matter if you keep your fingers together or not. But if you do keep them together, there is integration of hand and you can feel the energy better and easily make out whether the energy is less or more.

7. Don't cross your hands or legs while giving Reiki.

When Reiki channels are told not to cross their hands and legs while giving Reiki, people wonder what is meant by crossing.

The crossing of legs is not at the ankles or keeping legs in the lotus position (the position of meditation). What is really meant by crossing is keeping one leg over the other. In this position, you block the root *chakra*. This really does not block the energy flow. But this position also signifies that you are in a defensive position. Blocking the root *chakra* and solar plexus is a subconscious way of being defensive. We do this when we are sitting in a strange place, or talking to a stranger. We sit with one leg on top of the other and with arms folded at the solar plexus.

Because you are on the defensive in this position, it is suggested not to cross your hands or legs. You want to be as receptive as possible while giving Reiki. But even if you do cross either of them, it does not affect the energy flow.

8. What type of Reiki box should be used?
Some people say avoid using metallic box, while others support this because metal is a good conductor. Your Reiki box can be made up of anything. It can also be a purse, pouch, etc.

9. Being "successful" in healing.

There is no such thing as success in healing. It is really up to the energy to do the healing. Success and failure do not exist. Let the energy decide; you be a witnessing channel.

10. Experience of attunement.

Do not compare your experience with others. Don't assume if the other person experienced something you should also experience similar things. Also, don't get upset if you don't experience anything at all. Be receptive and in gratitude, always.

11. Reiki should not be given to the crown *chakra*.

As the crown *chakra* connects with intuition and spiritual issues, it does not really connect with physical diseases or organs. So, normally, we never give Reiki to the crown *chakra*. But we do give Reiki to it when healing addictions, mental retardation, neurological problems and when requesting guidance. It should also be healed in a person who is very sensitive to light.

12. How to use crystals.

Crystals are also called quartz. We mainly deal

with the clear quartz, i.e. the transparent or the near-transparent crystal. Crystals are amplifiers of energy, they can be charged and programmed. Programming is done according to the intentions, for example, you may program a crystal to clear a room, clear a block, energise a *chakra*, to send healing, etc., but they need to be charged regularly to maintain these programs. Because they can be programmed, they get easily affected by your aura and thoughts. So, anybody who will handle them will influence the crystal. If you have programmed a crystal, you should avoid letting others touch it. If you use the crystal occasionally and keep it in a closet most of the time, then it is good to wrap it in a silk cloth. This will prevent your programmed energy in the crystal from being dissipated.

It is not a good idea to keep crystals on the *chakras*. Their energy is very strong, while the *chakras* have subtle energy, especially the upper *chakras*. So, keep the crystals about four inches away.

Besides clear quartz, people also use rose quartz and amethyst. Rose quartz mainly works with the heart *chakra* and amethyst works with the third eye and crown *chakras*. Additionally, amethyst also has the quality of reducing the effects of intoxication.

13. The second degree symbols should not be shown to first degree channels or to people who are not Reiki channels.

Disclosing symbols is not a sin. You can show them to people. Nowadays, they are also in the books. So, if you read a book before doing Reiki, you also see them. This rule comes from the old tradition of secrecy. If you show it to first degree channels, it is really useless for them, as they need to get attuned to the second degree to be able to use them and also understand how to do so.

14. Do the blocks that are present in a person come in the way of attunement?

The attunement transcends blocks. We all have blocks. In fact, most of the people come to do Reiki only when there is a disease or a problem. Reiki enables you to heal those blocks. So, do not feel that if you have blocks, attunement will not be done properly.

But if you feel feverish or physically weak, do not attend the Reiki seminar, rest for a few days, recuperate and then go and get attuned.

15. Which are the sensitive areas in the body?
Depletion takes place mainly in the heart, solar plexus, *hara* and in the area of adrenals. Hence, these should be treated regularly.

16. The fees.
I have already discussed this in the chapter on IIIB Degree.

In India, there is a lot of variation in the fees for each degree and a lot of people ask why this is so. Each teacher decides on what he should charge for his teaching. Some teachers hire halls to teach Reiki in or even conduct their seminars in five-star hotels. These are also the reasons why the fees vary.

There are different types of teachers for different students. Each student attracts to himself the teacher of his type.

The fee variation has to be accepted. There are people who feel that Reiki should not be so easily imparted and hence charge high. While others think that they should make it easily available to common man, so they charge less.

17. Attitude of gratitude.

You will have this only when you feel that your life is a blessing and not a burden. Don't force the attitude of gratitude on to yourself before or while doing Reiki.

Dr. Usui formulated this to make us aware about the gifts and blessings of Reiki. When you understand its value, you will naturally feel the gratitude.

The Myth of 21 Days

Almost all books and all teachers talk about a 21 days' gap between each degree. But no teacher really gives a proper explanation for this. All that they say is that after the attunement, cleansing takes place in each *chakra* and it takes three days for each *chakra* to get cleansed. So, 3 x 7 *chakras* = 21 days.

But if it takes three days for each *chakra*, why don't all *chakras* get cleansed simultaneously? This way you can have all *chakras* cleansed in three days.

Again, if it takes 21 days for the *chakras* and the central channel to get cleansed, then how do people start giving Reiki to themselves and others immediately after attunement? All feel the flow of energy immediately after the attunement.

This 21 days cleansing is a misconception. Even before being attuned to Reiki, you have access to the healing energy. The ability to channel is present in body and the healing energy is present in nature. But you have access to only about 5% of it. After the attunement, the capacity of the *chakras* to channel energy is increased. So, immediately after the attunement, you start to channel about 90% of this energy. From 90% to 100% will take a few days, as the energy is working on the *chakras* even after the attunement is done. To reach this optimum level of flow will take a few days, but this time varies for each person. 10% is not a significant amount of energy and you should not be bothered about this.

Although it is suggested that you take your own time in learning Reiki, after doing each degree, see how you feel, and when you are ready for the next degree, you can proceed. Some people learn the next day, some do so after 21 days, while some others do after about three months or even a year. All this should depend on your own judgement.

Some Examples of Affirmations

1. This is one of my favorite affirmations, given to me by one of my teachers.
   "I do not know what I had asked for, but if I had asked for pain, misery, suffering and blockages, then I release them now. I ask for guidance and the complete healing of my being. So it is. So it is. So it is."
2. If you have problems with your legs:
   "I release all fears associated with my future accomplishments. I ask for balance in my life and trust in my ability to accomplish it."
3. Addictions (smoking):
   "I release the need to smoke (so many) cigarettes everyday. I do not feel the need to smoke any more cigarettes. My body no longer longs for the gratification that comes with smoking. The need for smoking is replaced by a new hobby, activity, avocation... the things that I desired to do but thought that there was no time for.

Doing this new activity has completly filled the vacuum created by releasing the need to smoke."

(Drinking):

"I do not feel the need for intoxication as I have now developed the ability to see and accept things as they are. I now have a new way of seeing things — problems which have solutions, and despair that has hope. I now resolve to live, with my full consciousness, a fulfilled life."

4. Anything to do with the past:

"Let the event which has caused this situation/limitation/disease in my body be resolved. I release the event from my memory." OR "I can live with the memory of the event as I have developed an acceptance of it and understood the higher meaning in it. My body no longer reacts as it did in the past, to the memory of that event."

5. Phobias:

"I no longer have this mental program which was conditioned in my childhood. I let this energy wash away this pattern from my memory cells and let me have a fuller life without any limitations. I am no longer afraid of _____. I can easily do _____ without feeling afraid."

6. "I am moving into an unknown future and I know that only good can come to me. I have good health, happiness and peace of mind. I am accomplishing higher things in my life with every new venture/direction that I take."

7. "The litigation has been resolved and justice has been done to all. I no longer have any unresolved or pending matters. Everything is whole, complete and simple."

8. Relationships:
"We now have a better and deeper understanding in our communication. I know exactly how she/he feels and now it is the same for her/him. Now there are no misunderstandings. In the past, there was a need to control because of fear and lack of trust in my own ability to accomplish things, now there is no control or conditional love, as I release the need for others to behave as per my expectations. I

accept the individual, natural expression of this person as it is and also at the same time, feel no need to be manipulative in my behaviour. Our relationship is growing deeper, richer and more fulfilling with each day in every way."

9. Left shoulder:
   "I release any guilt or self-blame that I have regarding not executing my responsibility properly in the past. I did what was best according to my knowledge. I accept it as God's will and forgive myself. I ask for the guidance and strength to fulfill my future responsibilities."

10. Right shoulder:
    "I release all worry for future responsibilities and accept the blessing of living fully in the present. I now have faith in the security of the future and trust that all that I need to fulfill my future responsibilities will be provided at the right time."

11. Resolving hate for parents:
    "I understand that my parents are affected by their conditionings and fears. I am aware

of the changing times and thus understand the generation gap. I forgive my parents for their fear-choices that concern me. I see them as people who need compassion and love. I forgive them and I set myself free of hatred."

12. "I accept old age with grace. I no longer need to fight natural processes. I also understand that the body has immense abilities to rejuvenate itself. I start this process by releasing my limiting attitudes — releasing my body of unnatural habits of the past and accept a new way of living, which is simple and natural. I ask for grace for my body and the inner strength of my being to make it physically strong, flexible and agile. I ask for rejuvenation and enlightenment of each and every cell of my body."

13. "I let go of my past. I have a new life, a new found strength and worth. I ask for light in my new life."

14. "I let go of this person. I let this person move towards his/her life-work and I let myself move towards mine. We met for a brief time at the crossroads of our life

patterns. There is no need for attachment. My happiness does not depend on anything other than my individuality."

15. "My negative thinking/doubts are my thoughts and I can easily turn them around and make them positive. I have nothing to lose by believing in my positive thoughts."

16. "I am doing perfectly well in my interview. If it is for my betterment and the betterment of the company and all concerned, let me have this job."

17. "I now have a job in a company that is close to my house, the transport is not a problem at all, the work atmosphere is good and the colleagues are also helpful and authentic. The job is fulfilling and so is the pay. I and others are completely satisfied with my work."

18. "I ask for my higher self to send me an opportunity for a new job—a wonderful new position which uses my creative talents and abilities. I release the belief that the opportunities are limited. I am surrounded with opportunities at every stage in my life."

19. "I now have my own beautiful place to live in. My house is an extension of my individuality. It is warm, loving, caring and nurturing for all of us and everything in it. It is always filled with good luck and growth."

20. "I now realise the need to express. I now find new ways to express myself in fulfilling ways. Expression is my divine right."

21. "Every event is in time. All experiences are in time. Even this will pass. It is not permanent. No situation or circumstance is permanent."

22. "There is no success and there is no failure. It is an experience, a growth. If the results are not according to my expectations, I don't give up. Motivation is my basic life force."

23. "There is no need to control people. I ask for guidance to accomplish things for which I depend on others."

24. "I allow the love of my own heart to wash through me, cleansing and healing every part of my body."

25. "I am guided by divine intelligence. I don't let other people's fears and doubts affect me."

26. "I take responsibility for my every thought. I am aware that with each positive thought the body feels energised and that negative thoughts deplete the body of energy."

27. "I release scarcity thinking. I know that there is enough for everybody. Nature is abundant and so is everything in human life."

28. "I am safe and secure, for I am an eternal part of the universe. I cannot lose that which doesn't belong to me. There is no need to be afraid."

29. "I accept my death. I accept that I shall die one day. It is part of reality. Everything dies. The energy keeps on changing forms. I accept death as I accept my birth, my accomplishments, my body... all the things in my life. Life is a set of experiences and I have lived it fully."

30. "I accept my death. I accept the transient nature of my life. I resolve to live my life to the fullest, each and every day."